LIFE IN OLD LOWESWATER

Cover illustration: *The old Post Office at Loweswater* [Gillerthwaite]
by A. Heaton Cooper (1864-1929)

Life in Old Loweswater

Historical Sketches of a Cumberland Village

by

Roz Southey

Edited and illustrated by Derek Denman

Lorton & Derwent Fells Local History Society

First published in 2008

ISBN-13: 978-0-9548487-1-2
ISBN-10: 0-9548487-1-3

Published and Distributed by L&DFLHS
Beech Cottage, High Lorton
Cockermouth, Cumbria CA13 9UQ
www.derwentfells.com

Designed by Derek Denman
Printed and bound in Great Britain
by CPI Antony Rowe

LIFE IN OLD LOWESWATER

Historical Sketches of a Cumberland Village

Contents

Life in Old Loweswater

List of Illustrations

* These images are taken from the Marshall family client records deposited in the Cumbria County Council Record Office at Whitehaven, reference CRO/W/D/WM11. The Society wishes to thank Waugh & Musgrave, Solicitors, of Cockermouth, for permission to reproduce these records, and the Archive Service of Cumbria County Council for assistance with the research for this book.

Roz Southey

Cold Keld in Loweswater, c. 1960

PREFACE

by Dr. Roz Southey

It's difficult not to be interested in history when the people of the past have left their names on the windows of your house. Who was the Ann Fisher who scratched her name in flourishes and curlicues on the glass in 1804? Who was the Thomas Smith who had much smaller and neater handwriting? I grew up in a house that reeked of history.

My parents moved to Loweswater in 1958 when I was six years old. The house we moved to, Cold Keld, was in need of renovations - just the thing to appeal to my father's practical instincts; over the years he replaced large parts of the roof, re-rendered the front of the house, put in fires and took them out again, painted and repainted, installed electricity. And in the course of this work, we came across hints as to the history of the house: carpenter's marks on roof timbers, blocked-up doorways, painted false windows, added partition walls. In the end, I succumbed to curiosity and went off to the Record Office in Carlisle to see if any documentary information survived to date the house.

It was at this point that I realised that the Record Office was crammed with documents about Loweswater and the surrounding area: manor records, parish records, council records, individual diaries ... It was all too good to keep to myself; I started writing articles for the parish paper.

The interest was immediate. Not only did people express their enjoyment of the articles, but they also started offering their own memories and memorabilia. Boxes of documents started coming out of lofts; Clem Storr of Thackthwaite generously allowed me to sift through piles of documents about Mockerkin School, other people brought out old savings books, or Show programmes, or invited me to check out the inscriptions in their houses. Someone pointed me in the direction of the large numbers of Quaker documents still remaining in London.

In the end, I wrote articles over a sixteen-year period. I moved away from Loweswater to get a job in Carlisle (which was handy for the Record Office), and then married and moved to Durham. Eventually, of course, I ran out of material and reluctantly gave up writing the articles.

Well, I say I ran out of material, but I still have enough notes on Mockerkin and Loweswater schools to write a book. I have files full of local wills, and copies of the parish registers and family trees of local families. Perhaps one day I'll sort them all out. In the meantime, I hope these articles are as enjoyable to read as they were to write.

Durham, March 2008

Loweswater by Edward Lear, 1837 by permission of the Wordsworth Trust, Grasmere

INTRODUCTION

This book is unusual in that people who spend their childhood in an area tend to accept it as normal and familiar, no matter how unusual the area and its people may seem to others. It is more often the offcomers to the Lakes who are stimulated to discover how the area developed its special qualities, through a millennium's interaction between people and the natural environment. But they usually start with landscape or houses. Perhaps only those brought up in this area can have a sufficient understanding of its people, through being a part of it, to approach a local history study by putting the people first. And history is about people.

Roz Southey's parents, the late Charles and Edna Williams, came to Roz's birthplace, Workington in Cumberland, from south-west England. In 1958, when Roz was six, they settled at Cold Keld in Loweswater, an old farmstead on the Thackthwaite road.[1] Roz attended school in Workington; then at Cockermouth Grammar before taking a history degree in Hull. More recently she was awarded her doctorate for her work on eighteenth century music and musicians, at the University of Newcastle, where she now lectures part-time.

The articles appeared in either the Loweswater Parish Papers, encouraged by the then vicar, Geoff White, or later in the Link of the combined benefice. The research was mostly done in the 1970s while Roz was living in Carlisle and was helping her father to uncover the history of Cold Keld. The articles formed a series of short, self-contained pieces, where the writing and often the narrative approach were as important as the local history content. There is a sense of discovery, a personal involvement and an apparent immediacy of writing that is not found in, say, a structured and systematically researched parish history. That is what makes the articles so attractive to anyone with a connection to Loweswater, but it leaves those readers with a definite risk of wishing to know more about local history.

In reprinting the collected articles for Lorton & Derwent Fells Local History Society, we had to agree whether they should be printed as they were or updated, revised, referenced, or joined together. We decided to leave the articles just as they were written, but to group them thematically, add notes where necessary, and some additionally supportive material for those who wish to have more context or to go further.

The society, the author and the editor wish to thank all those who have contributed to this book, and are grateful to the Council of the Civil Parish of Loweswater for their donation of £100 towards the cost of printing.

---

[1] L&DFLHS Journal No. 41 Feb 2008 contains Roz's Loweswater recollections.

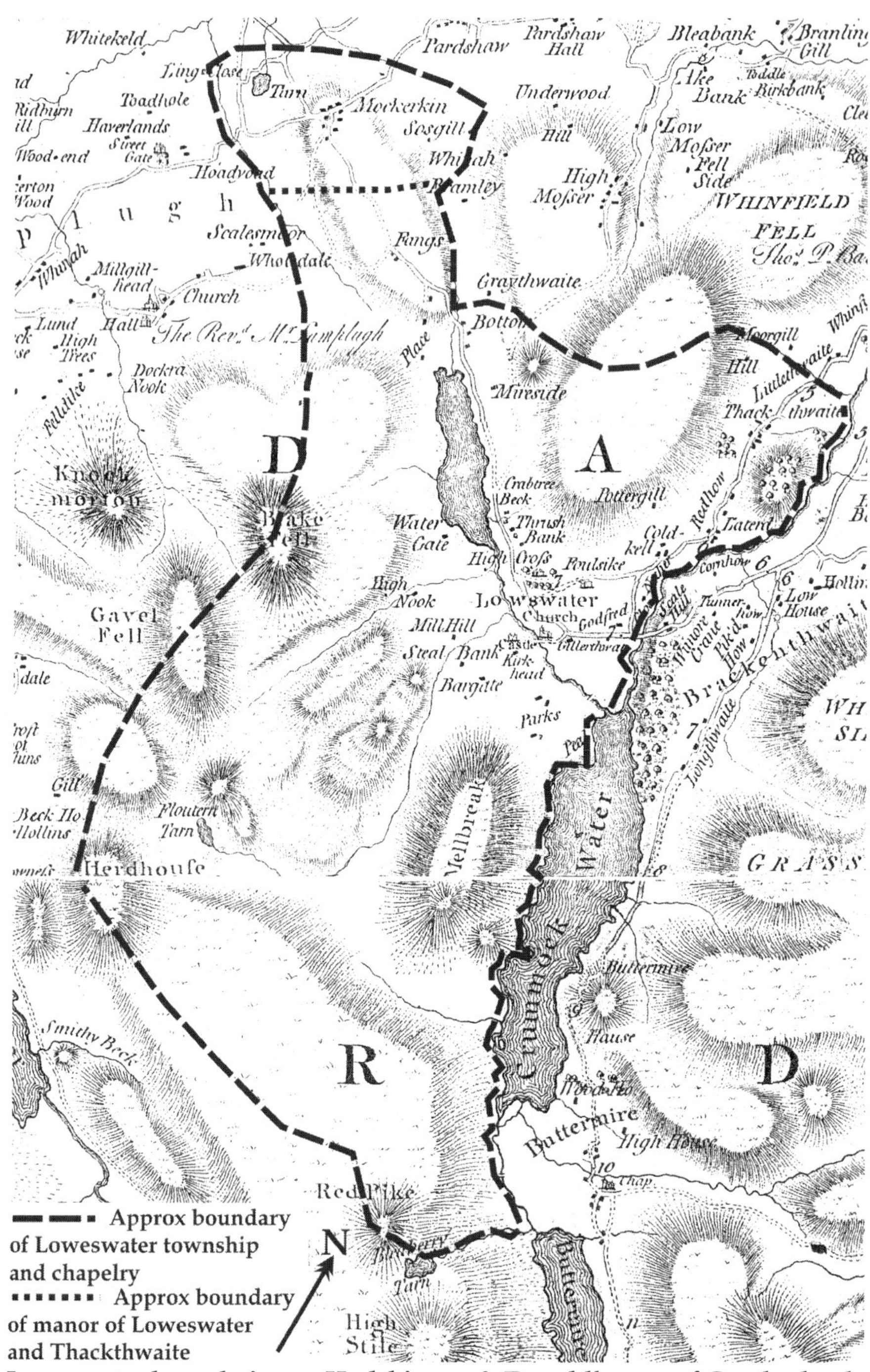

Loweswater boundaries on Hodskinson & Donald's map of Cumberland, surveyed 1770-1. Thomas Donald was buried in Loweswater.

Chapter 1: VILLAGE LIFE

What is Loweswater, who lived there and what was life like? The following group of six articles addresses these topics, though from different perspectives and at different periods. Life in past times includes birth and death as natural occurrences within the village, managed by its community.

A sequestered land starts with the tourists' view of the native inhabitants from 1793/4; which as we recall was the best of times and the worst of times, and a time when a thousand or two persons of 'rank and fashion' excluded from the dangerous continent, stayed in Keswick and passed through Loweswater via the Scalehill Inn on the Picturesque Tour. At Loweswater they hoped to see the true residual English yeoman families, who would fight the French rather than copy them. *Taking account of Loweswater*, a century later, is an analysis of the administrative census, from an internal village perspective. Much had happened since 1794, particularly in the mobility of the people, in that Loweswater was no longer sequestered, if it ever was, and fewer people spent their whole lives there. In the eighteenth century the population of Loweswater depended on what its land could produce, as illustrated by *Food glorious food.* Most families depended on their own arable land, a few cattle and an income from the sale of wool or cloth from a flock of sheep. By 1881, well into the railway age, much of the recent mobility of people was related to a large shift to pastoral farming and a consequent rural depopulation, plus the special but temporary factor of lead or iron mining.

Throughout the period covered, birth, life and death in Loweswater would not have changed much, but with a demographic mix very different from today. In the Loweswater of 1841, 37% were children, of 14 or under, and only 7% were 60 or over, and most of them had to earn their keep. Infant mortality was high, but the survivors had a good chance of a healthy adult life, because it was in the industrialising towns where mortality was highest and the poor had to go to the workhouse. But life in Loweswater was in no way idyllic or sanitised; accidents happened, natural disasters occurred as in *An amazing flow of water* in Brackenthwaite and were taken as part of life, though sometimes it was necessary to explain them by invoking the irrational, as in *The apprentice.*

A SEQUESTERED LAND[1]

William Hutchinson, a Durham man, wrote a guide to the Lake District and published it in 1794, to help visitors who were for the first time coming to this remote area of Britain. He quotes a slightly earlier traveller, Housman, who makes life in Loweswater seem idyllic.

> *I found,* [Housman says], *'a number [of inhabitants] who ... had seldom travelled beyond their sheepheafs, had seen no people but their neighbours and no country but their vales and surrounding mountains – their ideas are simple and their notions confined to narrow rules of nature: yet honesty, integrity and heart-felt happiness are no strangers to this sequestered land. The people live in harmony and they express contentment.*[2]

Life was not idyllic of course. It could be hard and short. It is possible, however, by combining Hutchinson's incomparably detailed account with church registers and newspaper snippets to put together a vivid and balanced picture of that life was like in the parish in the second half of the 18th century.

Physically, the valley must have looked much as it does today. Hutchinson describes it thus: 'On the sides and skirts of [the] fells grow several trees and much brushwood which affords great ornament to the landscape ... The fences are chiefly of brushwood and earth mounds, wherein many trees grow of different kinds. The inclosures are pretty regular and buildings are uncommonly good upon the whole.' The soil he describes as 'light and gravelly'.

The fields, he says, produced much oats and potatoes, a little barley and some wheat. He was surprised that few farmers grew turnips 'although the soil seems proper'. Much butter and cheese was produced in the parish.

In the matter of livestock, Hutchinson estimates that there were about 5,700 sheep in the parish; six of their fleeces weighed a stone, he says, and sold for 7s.6d. Horses were 14½ hands high and the local black cattle weighed 10 stone a quarter.

A study of the figures Hutchinson gives for the value of land in Loweswater and surrounding parishes gives a slightly less favourable picture of agriculture in the valley. Hutchinson says that there were two or three estates in the parish worth about £100 a year but most were worth

---

[1]First published December 1988-January 1989.

[2] Hutchinson 1794 Vol. II p.135. Hutchinson's history became the key reference work for Cumberland. John Housman was the son of Henry Howard's gardener at Corby Castle, Cumwhitton. He supplied extensive notes for the history, and his own descriptive tour was published in 1800. Ed.

about £20-£40. The average rent per acre of land in the parish was fourteen shillings. This compares with an average in Lorton of sixteen shillings (but less in Buttermere). Land near Keswick was valued at forty to fifty shillings an acre and even the poorer land in Crosthwaite parish was valued at twenty shillings. Bassenthwaite parish had some very poor land worth only five shillings, but most of the parish was worth twenty shillings an acre. This clearly makes Loweswater the poorest parish in the area.

This was reflected in the curate's wages. According to Hutchinson, the curate was supposed to receive a yearly salary of about £30 a year, again low compared with surrounding parishes. This salary was paid by the local inhabitants and the curate from 1742-1795, Thomas Cowper, only a year after he arrived, complained that he did not receive all the money he was entitled to 'by reason of ye Quakers, who refuse to pay or be distrained upon for ye accustomed annual interest'[1] He estimated that there were twenty Quaker families in the parish, out of a total [my estimation] of 75-80 families (approximately 370-400 people). Fortunately, the other inhabitants rallied round to make up the deficit.

Cowper was described by Hutchinson as 'a very respectable character, to whom Goldsmith's description of the village curate is very applicable'. ('A man he was to all the country dear/ and passing rich with £40 a year'/ Remote from towns he ran his godly race,/ Nor e'er had changed, and wished to change his place.')[2] He married four years after his arrival in the valley and he and his wife, Faith (born Faith Sumpson of Lorton) had two children, a son and a daughter. In 1770, his content must have been shattered by the death of his son, John, at the age of 19. The son's tombstone bears the only Latin inscription in Loweswater churchyard and incidentally illuminates his own teaching. John was, says his father, 'a sober and religious' youth and well-versed in the Latin and Greek languages and also philosophy.

The same subjects might well have been taught by Cowper to the sons of the better-off inhabitants of his parish; Loweswater might have been 'sequestered' but its people were not ignorant. As Housman admits: 'Many of the natives are people of property, of course have received a tolerable education and have been somewhat from home.' John Hudson of Kirkgate, Joseph Skelton of Foulsyke, and John Fisher of Cold Keld were all well-off men who considered themselves gentlemen.

Cowper, in his meticulously kept registers, gives an idea of the range of occupations in the parish. A casual glance reveals five weavers at High Park and several elsewhere, three shoemakers, four carpenters, two tailors, two blacksmiths (one at Mockerkin and one at Gillerthwaite – a

---

[1] Church registers.

[2] Oliver Goldsmith (1728?-1774) published his famous poem *The Deserted Village* in 1770. Ed.

pattern which endured for several centuries), one tanner and, rather enigmatically, a collier - Jacob Robinson at Red Howe. These activities were probably combined in most cases with some farming. Despite the fact that Loweswater was a comparatively poor parish, these people between them found the money to reroof the nave of the church in 1751 and the chancel in 1753 'at which time also a great part of the church was plastered'. In 1778, the church was flagged and paved (most churches and chapels of the time had earth floors) and a new reading desk made. It was a pious age.

More money had to be laid out, perhaps reluctantly, for the poor of the parish, like Jane Mirehouse of Pottergill who died in 1741. Jane had been born Jennet Iredell of Latterhead in 1666, was married at the age of 15 and widowed twice by the time she was 40) and Robert Pearson of Fangs 'a poor man maintained by ye Parish'. William Woodvil, a native of the parish who had moved to Carlisle, left £50 to be distributed to the poor of the parish yearly on St Thomas's Day, and Mary Mirehouse of Mockerkin in 1782 endowed a school on Howe Common so that ten poor children could be educated. The number of pupils usually exceeded ten.

One thing Cowper's registers show clearly is how hard and short life could be. He records a high proportion of deaths in infancy and in childbirth and considerable numbers of people dying in their late teens and early twenties. The *Cumberland Pacquet* also details several early deaths. For instance, in an August edition of the paper from 1775: 'died the 7th inst. of a short and severe illness, Mr Jacob Hudson of Loweswater, a young man of great genius and much respected by his acquaintance'. He was 19. In the April 11th edition of 1776, the *Pacquet* recorded: 'died a few days ago at Mockerkin, Miss Mirehouse, in the 25th year of her age, the only daughter of Mr John Mirehouse of that place'. In the registers, only a month after his son's death, Cowper was recording, what what must have been a very heavy heart, the death of Sarah Hudson of Kirkgate, the daughter of his parish clerk. 'She and the said John Cowper,' wrote Thomas of Sarah and his son, 'were pleasant and lovely in their lives and in their deaths they were not divided; their graves being contiguous at the south west corner'. Sarah was 20 years old.

Elsewhere Cowper records the death of Thomas Griffin in 1747, 'drowned at Park Bridge', and young Anne, daughter of John Hunter of Low Park who was drowned there in 1766. In 1757, he notes that Ann Bank of Low Park, 'a charming singer of psalms,' had died aged 23, and devotes to her a verse of his own composing the first two lines of which run: 'Sweet Harmonist, who died in youthful days/thy life was one continued hymn of praise'. He took comfort in his own daughter, Faith, who married Thomas Towerson of Kinniside, Ennerdalem and brought all of her children back to Loweswater for her father to baptise. (The custom was for the wife to take the first child only back to the parish of her birth.) Cowper's pride shines through in every grandchild he records.

Cowper himself lived to old age, dying just a year after Hutchinson's compliment to him was published. No one could have known better the joys and sorrows, the advantages and disadvantages of living in what Hutchinson describes as 'as beautiful and romantic retirements as any part of Cumberland or the north of England'.

Gillerthwaite in the early twentieth century

TAKING ACCOUNT OF LOWESWATER[1]

On the night of 7 March 1881, a man called John Wilkinson set off to make his way round the parish of Loweswater. He started at Spout House, rode up past Waterend to take in Sosgill and Mockerkin, then came back down past Fangs and the lake, to Thrushbank and High Cross. He then visited Foulsyke, took the track to Pottergill then to Thackthwaite. He then came back via Latterhead and Oakbank before branching off towards Godferhead and Low and High Park. And coming back round to High Nook, Watergate and Miresyke. By the time he had finished his circle of the parish[2], he had asked questions at every door, spoken to at least one person in every household and had scribbled in his notebook details of every one of the 301 persons living in the parish that night. John Wilkinson was the enumerator for the census - and it is to be hoped he had a fine night for his job.[3]

There had been censuses since 1801 but the 1841 census had been the first to be more than a mere counting of heads. It asked for the name of every person, their age and sex, their occupation, also whether they had been born in the county. The 1881 census also asked for the relationship of every person to the head of the household and the exact place of birth.

Understandably, people were suspicious. Rumours abounded. The government, everyone said, wanted to use the census so that they could improve the collection of taxes. In 1841, fears were so great that people were deliberately missed off the census, ages were falsified or questions were answered with 'I don't know'. By 1881, people were beginning to accept the situation but poor John could still have met with some hostility.

The government principally wanted to use the census for the same reasons that the local historian nowadays wants to use it - to examine the structure of society, to see how many people there were in each age group, how large families were, whether people moved around a great deal. The 1851 census returns for Loweswater (now in the Public Records Office, in London) yield some surprises.[4]

What about that old tale, for instance, that people in country areas lived all their lives in one place, never moving more than a few miles from home? On the night of the census, there were four visitors in the parish, one being the Rev. Christopher Southey (son of the poet Robert), who was

---

[1] First published February/March 1988.

[2] While the word 'parish' was used loosely at the time, until 1886 Loweswater was a parochial chapelry within the Parish of St. Bees, and the task of the enumerator was to cover the township of Loweswater, see p. 2, which included Thackthwaite, Mockerkin and Sosgill. Ed.

[3] The only house missing from Wilkinson's survey was Cold Keld, then known as Oak Bank House; its occupiers, Jane and Mary Key, were away, staying with friends.

[4] Copies of the census enumerators' books from 1841 to 1901 are available at the Whitehaven record office, or online through Ancestry.co.uk Ed.

staying with his friend the Vicar of Buttermere who in turn lodged at Red Howe. This leaves a resident population of 387. A count shows that 193 of these people had been born in Loweswater and 194 outside the parish. Some of the incomers were from neighbouring places such as Brackenthwaite and Lorton, but others came from further afield, from Whitehaven, Workington, Plumbland, Penrith, Liverpool, Scotland and Ireland.

Nor were all these incomers spouses of local people; whole families had come in from outside. Of the 77 families recorded by the census, only ten were wholly local, that is, parents and children all born in the parish. In a further 23 families, one parent had been born in Loweswater. But in 44 families, both parents and some of the children came from outside.

In short, most of the people born in the parish were children whose parents had moved in from elsewhere and some families show signs of having moved frequently. For instance, the Lacklingson family of Thackthwaite was made up of John, 49 years old and born at Moresby, his wife, Dorothy, aged 40, born at Broughton, and six children. The oldest child had been born at Greysouthen, the next two at Mosser and the last three in Loweswater. Judging by the ages of the children, the family had lived in Loweswater for between five and seven years.

It is also a surprise to find that very few households were 'extended' to include parents-in-law, nieces, nephews and so on. Most families, it seems, consisted solely of parents and children, although a number of households had servants, both house and agricultural. Those families that were extended were usually headed by a widow or widower or a single man who clearly needed help. One or two families had obviously illegitimate grandchildren.

Perhaps the biggest surprise of all is to find how many children there were. Almost two thirds of the households had children under the age of 21 - and that excludes servants who were often very young. In fact the census shows that nearly half the population of the parish was under 21 and only 17% were over the age of 50. It seems that life was hard and exhausting and not too long. Prize for the oldest person living in the parish must go to Joseph Clark, a widower aged 89 who lived at Hill. It is sometimes difficult to judge relationships from the census but it seems that he lived with his son, John, a farmer - and with two grandchildren (not John's children), a lodger and one farm servant. The youngest inhabitant in the parish was John Jackson, aged one month, living at Thrushbank.

Most of the people living in the valley were of course farmers, farm labourers or their families. There were 33 farms in the parish, including two at Sosgill, 8 at Mockerkin and 2 at Thackthwaite. (This compares with a rough estimate of 28 in 1945 and 12 at the present day.) The largest farm was Godferhead (160 acres) and the smallest at Mockerkin (11 acres). Most farms seem to have been between 40 and 70 acres. But in addition to farmers and farm workers there was a variety of 'support' occupations. There were two blacksmiths: Thomas Armstrong living at Mockerkin, who employed his 15 year old son Joseph as an apprentice, and Robert Beck living at Gillerthwaite. Also at Gillerthwaite lived Robert's son, John, who was a joiner, and Isaac Tyson who was a cartright. John Tyson, who might have been Isaac's father, was a char and trout fisher.

Not far from Gillerthwaite, in the cottage at the bottom of Vicarage Brow, lived the Post Office messenger, Thomas Sancton, and his wife. Just a little further away, at Muncaster House, lived Lemuel Norman who may have been Isaac Tyson's employer. He is described in the census as a cartright, but as he was blind the business was probably carried on by his son William, who employed four journeyman (a man who had completed his apprenticeship). This was obviously a large and flourishing business.

At High Nook and at the nearby Peill lived two wallers, John and William Lancaster, both getting on in years, being aged 70 and 64 respectively. At Thackthwaite were two tailors - Henry Johnston, a 60 year old widower and, in a separate house, Isaac Johnston, who may have been his son.

Some of the trades were practised by families whose farms were very small and who obviously needed to supplement their income.[1] (Many families also took in lodgers.) At Thrushbank, for instance, John Jackson, a widower, had two daughters and seven sons, plus one grandson (little John, the youngest inhabitant) to support on a farm of 48 acres. He added to his income by shoemaking; his oldest son William helped in this. At Place, the married daughter of Joseph Walker helped support her parents, her two brothers, one sister and her own two children by dressmaking.

The two wealthiest households in the parish were clearly the Parsonage House and Foulsyke. The Vicar, the Rev Jeremiah Atkinson (aged 68) and his wife Frances lived in the Parsonage with their daughter Mary, their assistant housekeeper, Mary Ann Hodgson, two house servants, one labourer and a lodger. At Foulyske on the night of the census, Major and Mrs Brougham were absent from the parish but three female and one male house servants remained as did Jemina Johnston, the Brougham's 24 year old governess, and her two charges, James Brougham aged 6 and his sister, Mary Isabel, aged 5. Perhaps Jemina was friends with the local schoolmistress, Hannah Askew, who lived at the schoolhouse with her widowed mother; Hannah was only 19.

Unfortunately, the census may not be entirely reliable. After John Wilkinson scribbled down his notes on the night, they were copied neatly into larger books by someone else. John signed those copies as correct but mistakes could sometimes slip through. Was the family at Thackthwaite

---

[1] It may of course be that the farm land was merely used as a source of food to tide the workman over during times at which his first occupation was not sufficient.

really called Lacklingson for instance? Some errors were also corrected at this time but illegibly. In addition, there was nothing John could have done about people who lied to him on the doorstep, about their age for instance, or who glamorised their profession, or simply forgot the smallest servant or one of an abundance of children. But it is still possible to build up from the census an overall picture of what life was like in Loweswater in the middle of the 19th century - and fascinating to compare it with what we know of our own time.

Two views of a 'fiddle' used in 1958 to broadcast seed manually across the fields. Seed was fed from the bag into the wooden chute, which in turn fed it into the metal fan below. This was rotated by means of a bow, causing the seed to spray out across the field as the operator walked.

FOOD, GLORIOUS FOOD[1]

Everyday things like food and drink are so frequently taken for granted that they are rarely recorded – this article is therefore rather a dip into the soup of history, so to speak, rather than a three course meal.

The easy bit first. Drink. No doubt taverns have existed in the area virtually since it was inhabited; the first recorded instance dates from 1504, when Henry Burnyeat was fined 2d by the Lord of the Manor for allowing a house belonging to him to be used as a tavern. Mine host was one Elesabeth Tailyouse and one of her rivals was Catherine Jackson who ran a tavern from a house owned by Christopher Jackson (her husband?) Christopher was fined 2d too.

Elesabeth and Catherine sold ale though as most people brewed their own, the taverns were probably frequented more for the social aspects than the alcohol. In the 18th and 19th centuries each farmer would take his home-grown barley to one of the three local kilns or malthouses – at Deanscales, Eaglesfield and Whinfell Hall – to be made into malt for brewing.

If you wanted something a little different and did not mind paying for it, you could visit Scalehill Hotel in the 19th century for … wine and negus, rum and brandy, gin and whisky, punch, (and fruit, lemons and sugar) cyder and shrub (a cordial made from fruit-juice and spirits e.g. rum shrub), ginger beer and soda water, coffee and tea, ale, porter (a dark brown bitter beer blend brewed from charred malt) and the odd biscuit to mop it all up.

Tea was a relatively late arrival in this country. Rumour says that the first cup of tea ever brewed in the area was made in about 1780 by Hannah Dixon of Toddall in Whinfell, using a copper kettle she had been given as a child. The tea cost the enormous sum of seven shillings per pound. At the time, apparently, no one quite knew what to do with the brew – some people, it's said, boiled it up and ate the leaves, throwing the liquid away; some mixed the leaves with butter and spread it on bread while drinking the liquid. The last, rather strong, cup in the pot was mixed with a substantial amount of rum and given to the most favoured person present.

(Another Dixon of Toddall, by the way, owned the first umbrella in use in Whinfell – this was in the first half of the 19th century. It was red and he owned it for two years before he plucked up the courage to go out in public with it.)

As far as food is concerned, fragmentary glimpses can be gleaned, mainly from wills and diaries. Most families would provide nearly all their own food. Crops like barley for beer, oats for oatcakes, and potatoes and

[1] First published May 1992.

fruit were grown for home consumption and for market. John Walker of Thackthwaite, writing about his childhood in the first decades of the 19th century, remarks: 'Fruit was abundant. I have known apples and plums to be taken to market by the cartload.' When he talked of strawberries however, he was referring to the most popular type of potato grown locally. 'It was dry, mealy and fine-flavoured; red and white in colour, and even in size.' Alas, the variety was wiped out by disease in one, three or four years around 1826. At the time, potatoes were retailing from about 4d a stone.

Inventories accompanying wills only occasionally mention foodstuffs. The inventories of the goods of Jennet Pearson of Fangs and John Jenkinson of Waterend, both made in 1648, refer to salt and James Dickinson of Mockerkin is known to have possessed a pewter salt-cellar. Butter and cheese are often mentioned - obviously home produce - for instance in 1691 (inventory of William Mirehouse of Pottergill), 1699 (inventory of Phillip Burnyeat of Crabtreebeck) and 1700/01 (inventory of John Burnyeat of Thackthwaite).

Hens, sheep, cattle and pigs would provide meat for the family, although Thomas Fletcher of Thrushbank was a rare example of someone who did not keep hens. John Wilkinson's inventory of 1707 refers to 'beef, bacon, butter and cheese' (worth together 15s 6d); John Woodall's will of 1670 likewise mentions 'beefe and bacon'.

William Mirehouses's inventory of 1691 also mentions fish, presumably caught locally. Later, of course, fishing became sport rather than necessity; in 1853, for instance, Jonah Dixon went out with four other friends and caught 12 pike and one trout. Back in 1477, however, trout-fishing was illegal under any circumstances - William Harrison was fined by the Lord of the Manor for catching trout, strictly the Lord's property.

One other type of local produce should be mentioned although it may have been rare; the wills of John Woodville (1670) and his wife Jenet (1672) refer to bees - I know of no other references.

Early in the 19th century, the *Cumberland Pacquet* carried a remarkable story of festive cheer which deserves to be quoted in full:

> *As an instance of the great festivity which prevails at this season, a correspondent informs us that in the township of Buttermere (which consists of only 16 families) there are 17 fat sheep killed, from each of which sheep, 30 pies are to be made; so that the number of pies to be destroyed this Christmas in the township of Buttermere amounts to 510.*

Rather a monotonous diet.

And finally, as they say, rather more sumptuous fare for a Loweswater man who travelled further than most: Jonah Dixon of

Waterend. The story of Jonah's travels require a little telling of background. Jonah's father, Jonathan, who was a widower, decided in the early 1780s to remarry - his housekeeper. This produced vehement condemnation as the lady does not seem to have been popular in the family. After bitter arguments, Jonathan's elder son, another Jonathan, flung himself dramatically out of the house, saying he was off to America and would never return. After two or three years, it became obvious that either the younger Jonathan meant what he said or that he was sulking, so Jonathan senior sent the younger son, Jonah, off to Philadelphia to bring his brother back home.

Jonah seems to have had a delightful time. He found his brother within a few days of his arrival in America in 1769, then clearly decided to have the holiday of a lifetime. He spent several months riding around the countryside, having adventures with tremendous thunderstorms and rickety ferry boats, visiting huge waterfalls and undertaking overnight horse rides alone in unknown country.

On 27 November, 1770, he 'took a walk to German town with Robert Dove and dined at a German's house, sign of King Geo the Third.' He and his companion had what he called 'a good harty dinner' with pork and 'cold alee' (suggestions as to what 'alee might be, are welcome - could he possibly have meant 'cole slaw?')

All this, however, wasn't quite satisfying enough because he immediately returned to Philadelphia and 'supped with Dove upon Barbacued [sic] Partridges and roasted potatoes'.

(If anyone is interested in the ending of this particular family saga - Jonah persuaded his elder brother to return home and make up the quarrel with his father. Jonathan junior quickly settled down in Loweswater again, married, had a family and was widowed. Then, just to prove the old adage about following in his father's footsteps, he married his housekeeper ...

The family of course did not approve at all.)

And it is reported that he was a great chewer of tobacco, a habit he had learnt in America.

AN AMAZING FLOW OF WATER[1]

The weather is supposedly the Briton's favourite topic of conversation. Notes on unusual falls of snow, or heavy storms, or huge hailstones frequently found their way into church registers. Thomas Cowper, curate of Loweswater from 1744 until 1795 made many such jottings. Newspapers too have always found that the weather makes interesting copy – the Carlisle Journal over the years recorded a number of such stories in connection with Loweswater.

For instance, there is the occasion when there were '16 miles of snowdrifts in Lamplugh' (February 15th 1895). 'A large gang of men', the Journal records, 'were engaged in putting the road heading from Lamplugh across to Loweswater, which is one of the most heavily blocked roads in the parish, the drifts in many places being 8 feet high, while at one place on the high road the snow was found to be 13 feet high'. Only four days later, the Journal was telling its readers that Curmmock Water was frozen over at the Scale Hill end and crowded with skaters from Cockermouth and the surrounding area. This was a time of rural depression and some unemployed men built an igloo on the frozen River Cocker and charged for entrance. According to the Journal, they earnt 'a good harvest of coppers'. It is to be hoped that they had all learnt from an incident of sixteen years before (reported in the Journal of January 17th 1878) when Hannah Scott and her niece Hannah Faulder fell through the ice while skating at Loweswater, an accident caused by the ice being covered with snow, preventing the women from seeing the difference between the old and new ice.

What might have been a tragedy very nearly turned into farce. 'They screamed for assistance,' says the Journal, 'but although they were observed from the shore, people dare not venture onto the ice'. By the time would-be rescuers had prepared ropes and ladders, aunt and niece had managed to save themselves by scrambling back out onto the ice. 'Both ladies were in a very exhausted condition and Mrs Scott's neck was cut by the ice but both are recovering.'

But by far the most dramatic of natural catastrophes occurred during Thomas Cowper's curacy in Loweswater, in 1760. Cowper's entry in the register however hardly hints at the extent of damage caused by a mysterious and still unexplained phenomenon. 'September 7th 1760, was happened ye floods on Brackenthwaite Fells which sanded over ye Ground at Langthwaite'.

The Gentleman's Magazine, published in London, carried a more comprehensive description of what happened, in an article entitled: 'An authentic account of a Water-spout which mostly fell upon Brackenthwaite'. The author, Robert Dixon, calls himself an eye-witness but he means by that

---

[1] First published October/November 1988.

that he saw the aftermath of the incident. Fortunately, the 'waterspout' occurred just after midnight, when everyone was safely in bed. (Dixon places the date of the spout on 19 September but there is no doubt that he and Thomas Cowper are referring to the same incident.)

Three streams were involved in the flooding according to Dixon, 'Lizza, Hopebeck and Habcorton', but the greatest damage was caused by the flooding of the Liza, a stream 'little more than sufficient to turn an ordinary mill'. Dixon suggests that 'breakings, or falls of water' affected the three streams high on the summit of Grasmoor sending torrents of water down the stream-beds. As the water cascaded down Grasmoor, it picked up vast quantities of rubbish, 'the whole side of the mountain down which it rushed with inconceivable rapidity, being covered with vast heaps of stones, beds of gravel, sand and earth, which lying loose were easily carried away'.

At first, little damage was caused as the Liza's normal course lay in a steep ghyll, where high rocky banks kept the water narrowly confined. As soon as the Liza came out onto Lanthwaite Green however, it started to wreak havoc. In the first field it came to, it swept away the soil down to the bedrock; in the second –a field of about ten to twelve acres – it 'laid down a layer of sand of such a thickness as never to be removed'. This is presumably the sand to which Cowper referred in the register. Dixon reports that when the floods receded, the old stream bed hereabouts – about five to six feet wide and one foot deep – was found to have been widened to about 18-20 yards wide and 1½ yards deep.

The water then spread out across the fields on Lanthwaite Green. It was still travelling very quickly and with such force that a wall a quarter of a mile from the stream-bed was knocked down and swept away. The current dug huge holes in the ground and filled them up again with stones and sand carried down from Grasmoor. One pit, left unfilled, was later measured at 800-10000 yards in area and about 8 feet deep. When the stream bed narrowed, the water again picked up speed and stripped more fields, leaving behind another thick later of sand. It carried away trees from a wood, two stone bridges, and a causeway 'of prodigious breadth', supported by a most enormous bank of earth. In short, Dixon says, 'Nothing which fell in its way was able to resist it: but earth, trees, hedges, stones, walls, bridges, piers and mounds were swept away'. Eventually the torrent swept into the River Cocker which burst its banks and overflowed. This flooding, however, was over more level ground and took much of the force out of the water. The worst danger was over.

The following day, inhabitants surveyed the damage. By some miracle, no houses had been damaged, though there had been two narrow escapes. The mill near Low House, which the Liza normally operated, had been saved by rock which had deflected the course of the torrent toward the opposite bank, and a second house, unnamed, ended on a little island – 'the ground being all carried away to a considerable depth within two yards of it, where the solid rock began, on which the house was founded'. No doubt the Reverend Mr Cowper could not resist pointing out Biblical references relevant to the situation.

Robert Dixon attempted in the following days to discover the quantity of water involved, without much success owing to the large number of variables involved. He quotes very seriously: 'A Clergyman in the neighbourhood' [Mr Cowper?] who had remarked that 'all the water of Crummock ... could not have done half so much harm' and gives measurements of Crummock so readers can work out the calculations for themselves. Dixon measured the depths of holes and channels and the height of water marks on houses; one high water mark was 12 feet above ground level on a house about 30 yards from the normal course of the stream.

'With regard to the physical cause of this uncommon phenomenon,' Dixon quotes two theories which had been put to him. One – that the water spouts on top of Grasmoor had been caused by high winds – he discounted immediately as there had been very little wind during the preceding day and what little breeze there was had died down before evening. Neither was he happy with the second suggestion that 'an extraordinary rarefaction of the air by igneous meteors' was the culprit. As he pointed out: 'there was not the least lightning seen or thunder heard, not the other diagnostic of the atmosphere being charged with a more than ordinary stock of sulphurous exhalations, and nitrous acids, at that time'. So it seems that the exact cause of what the Gentleman's Magazine calls 'a most surprising flow of water' will forever remain a mystery.

UNNATURAL CAUSES[1]

The case of Robert Thompson who was murdered in Loweswater in 1524 has been mentioned in these articles before. As usual, only half the story has survived so the circumstances of the murder are not known nor whether the accused murderers, Richard Newcom of Rannerdale and a friend, a Mr Peill, were ever caught and convicted. Almost exactly a century later (1626), another murder took place but this time it is the victim who is likely to remain unknown; a court record only informs us that Thomas Jackson of Thackthwaite was 'attainted of felony and executed for murther', all his 'dyvers goodes, household stuff and corne' were forfeited and given to the Lord of the Manor, Henry Patrickson.

Murder has, thankfully, been rare in Loweswater but violent or mysterious death has not. Coroner's records give details of at least 23 inquests conducted on deaths in and around Loweswater and Buttermere between 1757 and 1873.

Some of these deaths were, so to speak, false alarms, deaths that looked suspicious but which in fact had a natural explanation. Such was the death of Ann Wilkinson in 1847; she was found dead in her house and the verdict was apoplexy (probably a stroke). Natural causes too was the verdict on Dan Jenkinson who died in July 1791. In his case, however, there were contributing factors; the Coroner's jury decided he died of 'natural causes after wrestling and drinking'.

Road accidents occurred from time to time, though rarely - only two, in 1820 and 1852, are recorded, both involving a fall from a horse or cart. In addition (though this case does not appear in the Coroner's reecords), John Fisher of Cold Keld fell from his horse at Armathwaite near Bassenthwaite in 1905 and died soon afterwards from his injuries. Slightly more common - three cases in twelve years - were accidents in the slate quarries, generally caused by unexpected falls of stone.

These latter can best be described as industrial accidents; the saddest in this category took place in 1839, not in the slate quarries but in Loweswater's only mine, the lead mine near Netherclose.

This was a spectacularly unsuccessful venture, but as long as it remained open it employed almost 200 miners and boasted a very large waterwheel underground, used to pump water from the workings. Like all mines at the time it employed children, who crawled into spaces too small for an adult. One of the children was ten year old William Fearon whose father Joseph was also a miner. One day, William was evidently trying to retrieve metal that had fallen under the crushing mill; in the process, he came into contact with the moving waterwheel and was knocked aside. He

---

[1] First published October 1993.

hit his head against the crank post of the crushing mill and died almost immediately.

Loweswater, contrary to some beliefs, has not been untouched by events in the wider world. Even before this century's wars, three natives of Loweswater may have died in battle.

In 1704, John Winder of Mockerkin was granted an administration order for the estate of his son, another John, who had died 'in the Warrs'. Was this in the Battle of Blenheim, in Bavaria, where the Duke of Marlborough, amongst others, halted the French advance on Vienna? At the end of the same century, there is a trace of mystery surrounding the death in 1785 of David Harrison, son of Jonathan and Eleanor Harrison, again of Mockerkin; his parents' gravestone in Loweswater churchyard says simply that he 'perished at sea near the Isle of Whitehorn'. This could have been an accidental death but that of his elder brother twenty years later was more likely not. Thomas Harrison was Captain of H.M.S. Dromedary in the middle of the Napoleonic Wars; he died in 1805 - but six months before the year's crucial battle, Trafalgar.

The Coroner's records detail only two cases of suicide (though it is possible that other cases were passed off as natural deaths). The records do not tell the sad background to these stories; we know only that in February 1845, Mary Lightfoot of Buttermere poisoned herself with white arsenic; 28 years later, Thoms Mitchell of Thackthwaite hanged himself. Both were in their late 20s; in Thomas's case, the verdict was 'temporary insanity'.

By far the largest category of deaths investigated by the Coroner was that of drowning. In fact, the earliest recorded untimely death in Loweswater (this one detailed in the Manor Court records) is a case of drowning; in 1509, the Curate of Loweswater, Richard Robyson was fined 6s. 8d. by the Manor Court for slandering the 'inquisition' into the death and disposal of the goods of Janet Wilkinson 'recently drowned there'.

Many of the cases the Coroner dealt with were tragic tales of lost children. In 1808, little Isabella Clark, aged 8, and her elder sister, Jane, aged 9, were drowned in Stockbeck. In 1898 another child drowned at Thackthwaite; McDonald Martin, aged 9, was playing with his brother and a friend when he slipped off a footbridge over the River Cocker. His body was found a day later at Rogerscale. The youngest victim was three year old Christopher Graham of Netherclose who wandered away from his mother and was found drowned only minutes later in a washtub that held four inches of water.

Some of the drowning cases are touched with farce. John Wilson of Mockerkin went to market in Cockermouth and celebrated with some heavy drinking, confident that his horse would carry him home without guidance. But the horse was thirsty too, and stopped to drink from a stream - John Wilson slid over its neck into the water and never got out again.

But most drownings happened in the lakes and in the late 18th century unwary tourists suffered most. A typical case was that of Alexander Farmer, a 20 year old visitor from West Hartlepool. In 1897, he paddled out too far in Crummock Water and lost his footing as the lake bed suddenly dipped. He was accompanied by two cousins but neither could swim and were forced to watch helplessly as he was carried away.

For some, there were lucky escapes. In January 1879, Hannah Scott and her niece, Hannah Faulder, went skating on Loweswater Lake which had frozen over. Unfortunately, there had been a fresh fall of snow which disguised the difference between old and new ice; new thin ice gave way beneath them and they plunged into the freezing water. Spectators in the bank were too nervous to venture onto the ice but hurriedly began to put together makeshift ladders to reach them. Before they could reach the women, however, Hannah and her niece had saved themselves, struggling exhausted onto the ice. Their only injuries were a few scratches to Hannah's neck.

Curiously Crummock Water gave back what it had taken as if the lake itself was mourning. In 1833, a boatman was rowing a party across the end of the lake to visit Scale Force. One of the ladies in the party, idly staring into the clear water, saw an object glittering. The water was over a yard deep, but the boatman managed to dredge up the object. It was, they discovered, a lady's mourning ring.

THE APPRENTICE[1]

It used to be the custom to tell ghost stories late at night on Christmas Eve. This is the nearest Loweswater comes to a ghost story; it is a tale of the supernatural really and was reported by the Cumberland Pacquet on 22 December 1774. The paper protects the people involved by mentioning no names, so we will call the boy in the story Will and his employer Mistress Pearson.

Will lived at Buttermere and was apprentice to a shoemaker. The shoemaker no doubt was an inoffensive little man who applied himself to his work and left his wife to manage the apprentices and the business side of his trade. Less than two weeks before Christmas 1774, Mistress Pearson sent Will out on an errand.

It was a dreary, drizzly day and on the mountains the mist sank lower and lower. As Will trudged along rough tracks to isolated houses to deliver his packages, the mist drifted around him and soaked his clothes and stuck the ends of his hair against his cheeks. As the youngest of the apprentices, Will was often sent out on such errands and was used to tramping for miles in all weathers but after a while, such dreary weather began to depress even his spirits. He tried to whistle and even to sing but the mist echoed his singing and made him start. He began to hurry and longed to be home.

His trip that day meant walking about five or six miles over roads that in those times were little more than muddy tracks, Will walked faster and faster, following the dark track into the thickening mist, longing for a glimpse of familiar landmarks. He began to wonder if he was still on the right road and several times hesitated over a side track. But he kept straight on and eventually saw ahead of him the hump-backed sides of a bridge.

He gasped with relief as he recognised the bridge. Not far to go. He was almost running now. His hair was sodden and trickling water down the back of his neck. As he came onto the bridge, he stubbed his toe against a large stone and clutched at the parapet of the bridge.

It was probably that stone that saved his life. As he clutched at the parapet, he was suddenly buffeted by a great gust of wind. It blew him against the side of the bridge; for a moment he looked down into rushing, white-flecked water and was certain that he would be blown over. He held on to the parapet for dear life and at last the wind dropped. Shaken, he stumbled back off the bridge onto the track.

There was no wind, not even the slightest breeze ruffling the drifting mist.

---

[1] First published December 1987-January 1988: This was also published in *Cumbria* Magazine, December 1989, pp.612-22.

He *could not* go back onto that bridge. He *could not* cross it. He was convinced that if he tried to cross it again, he would be blown over the edge and drowned. But how was he to get home?

In the end, he tramped an extra three miles, still shaking, so that he could reach home without crossing that river. As, at long last, he approached Buttermere and his master's house, he was almost in a state of collapse.

Mistress Pearson snatched open the door and confronted him with a face of fury. 'And where have you been? Don't you know there's work ...' But then she bent and peered into his face. One plump hand landed in the small of his back and propelled him towards the fire. A cup of hot broth was thrust into his hands and he found himself telling her everything.

It was not to be expected that Mistress Pearson would believe him. She chuckled a bit and clucked a lot and finally shook her head in exasperation. But she was not unkind.

'Foolish child,' she said. 'I'll warrant you never go near *that* bridge again. Now be off with you and change out of your wet clothes. Oh, and call the other lads to dinner.'

With overwhelming relief, he clattered upstairs and she heard his voice calling to the other apprentices.

What with making sure the dinner was cooked and the lads had washed their hands and calling her husband *three* times and serving up the broth and bread, it was a little while before Mistress Pearson realised that Will hadn't come downstairs again. Only a little worried, she sent one of the other boys to look for him. A moment later, she heard the boy cry out –

There was an inquest of course. The boy nervously told the Coroner that he had found Will sitting on one of the stairs, strangled in the crupper of a saddle which hung in the staircase. The Coroner was baffled; it was almost unaccountable, he said, how anyone could be suffocated in such a posture. Everyone agreed that Will was the most cheerful of lads and would not under any circumstances have laid 'violent hands upon himself'.

The verdict was 'accidental death'. But Mistress Pearson thought otherwise.

Chapter 2: MAKING A LIVING

Most families in Loweswater were headed either by a yeoman farmer who owned and worked his own farm or tenement, or increasingly by a farmer who rented the tenement from the landowner. In either case they lived off their own produce, both arable and pastoral, and in the earlier eighteenth century they would have spun their own wool and made their own clothes, using the services of the websters of Peil to weave the woollen cloth and the fuller at Bargate to waterproof and shrink it. Much surplus cloth would have been sold. Cornmillers, blacksmiths, carpenter/wheelwrights, and waller/builders provided for local needs.

This group of article addresses the other rural industries which were important to Loweswater's people. Access to timber and underwood was always a source of dispute, and caused increasing problems as the commons were gradually denuded and kept that way by grazing stock. Timber trees were the property of the lord, even on a customary tenant's tenement, and could be cut down for essential purposes only with the lord's permission. But a tenant could pollard trees on his land for structural timber and could grow coppice on enclosed land, free of stock. Coppice provided charcoal, poles, hurdles, baskets, oak bark for tanning and much more, as covered in *Seeing the woods and the trees* and *The rewards of industry.*

All Lakeland villages had stone quarries for local use, but mining had to follow the mineral veins. The successful Loweswater lead mines, at Nether Close, and later between Whiteoak and High Nook becks, were on the lines of the veins which appear at Force Crag and at Stoneycroft in the Newlands Valley. The proposed iron mines described in *Iron in them thare hills* were not so successful. But mining left us some good level roads in the Loweswater Fells.

Fishing always provided an important part of the Lakeland diet, and potted char was 'exported' well before the tourists came, but when they did come they expected to fish, to be served fish and to take away fish. In the nineteenth century the Lord of the manor of Loweswater, John Marshall Esq. of Leeds and Hallsteads on Ullswater, either owned or had the fishing rights of all three lakes, as well as ownership of Scalehill Inn, most woodland in Loweswater, Buttermere and Brackenthwaite, and the mineral rights of all Loweswater. So it is not surpising that he is often *On the hook* in these articles.

SEEING THE WOOD AND THE TREES[1]

If you glance at one of the charters granted to the Monks of St Bees Priory, you'd think that the whole of Loweswater was once as wooded as the Amazon basin; the monks were given permission to pasture their cattle in the 'forest' there. It is likely, however, that 'forest' was used in the medieval sense of an area of country where forest laws applied and which enclosed not only trees but extensive clearings, arable land and villages.[2] It is difficult to estimate how wooded the parish really was; certainly 'Loweswater' means the 'leafy lake' which suggests a surround of trees then as now. The name 'Coledale' also implies an area of woodland. It means 'the valley of the charcoal burners' and those men worked in the heart of the wood which supplied their raw material. They needed vast quantities of trees and it is probable that woods along the shores of Crummock Water must have been extensive.

The woods belonged to the Lord of the Manor and it was an offence to cut down trees without his permission. Laws are only made to be broken, it seems, and many were the people taken to the manor court for his particular 'crime'. From the court's records, we get glimpses of the types of trees which grew in the valley - oak and alder, 'mastic' trees (meaning a tree yielding resin) and cherry trees. 'Hollins' means 'the place where holly bushes grow' and the fact that this was significant enough to name a place, suggests that holly was perhaps not all that common. 'Crabtreebeck' is self-explanatory.

There were a variety of reasons for offences against the law. The utilitarian was most common; wood was of course a building material. (It was not used extensively for fuel, peat being used instead.) Here, unfortunately, the Lord's tenants found themselves in a difficult situation. In 1523, for instance, James Jackson's wife was fined at the manor court for 'having a ruinous house for want of repairs to the roof'; the following year, William Iredale was warned that his roof should be mended before the Feast of St John the Baptist or he would be fined six shillings and eight-pence. Yet, not very much later, James Dalton - trying to repair three houses recently burnt down - found himself being fined for cutting down 'small oaks and other forbidden material' for that purpose. It hardly seems fair.

Of course, there was the profit motive too. Judging by the fact that Thomas Wilkinson of Brackenthwaite did not turn up at the Manor Court in 1481, it is likely that he did not want too close an enquiry into why he had cut down a number of oaks. In 1521, John Bank of Brackenthwaite was in

---

[1] First published in January 1993.

[2] The essential component of a forest was deer, and the priority of its management was providing free chase for the lord. Ed.

trouble for cutting down alder, mastic and cherry trees – which he had sold to the Prior of Carlisle to use in the building of a lime kiln. A few years later, John Robynson of Park cut down various trees to make two small carts which he then sold to 'foreign' persons, i.e. residents of Ullock and 'Withmyr'.

By 1619, this was one of a number of issues that caused violent arguments between Lord and tenants. An agreement of that year between Loweswater's inhabitants and the Lord, Anthony Patrickson of Patterdale, mentions a 'controversy' for 'several years past' over 'their customary claims ... to some part of their wood growing upon their tenements within the said manors'. After much negotiation, the tenants were granted permission to use all the woods and individual trees on their tenements as they saw fit or needed to, excepting only woods 'on a parcel of ground called the Bank and another in Bargate between the low yeat on the east side of Gillbeck – parcel of the tenement of Peter Walker'.

This probably did not give the tenants a great deal of woodland to use; records for the 17th century are sparse but the tithe map of 1839 shows very little woodland on most farms. Gillerthwaite, Askhill and Miresyske had less than an acre of woodland each and Bargate, with the Lord's Wood, only 2½ acres. Some farms (Bargate and Miresyke included) had 'wood meadow' – usually a wood into which animals had at some stage been turned to graze. The animals ate the young seedlings presenting the wood from regenerating and turning it into a field with a large number of trees.

Nevertheless, the woodland in the landscape was an important resource and, as usual, it was the Lord of the Manor who benefited, being the owner of the valley's large expanses of woodland such as Lanthwaite Wood and Holme Wood. The papers of John Marshall in the 1830s and 1840s contain numerous references to these woods.

The usual practice was to coppice the woods, cutting down most of the trees while quite young and allowing suckers to sprout from the stumps or 'stools'. These suckers or poles would eventually be cut down allowing more to grow in their turn. Each stool would be cut once in a period ranging from seven to fourteen years. The crop of thin-ish young trees resulting from coppicing like this were known as 'underwood'. In addition certain trees in the wood would be allowed to grow to maturity to provide timber for large purposes such as rafters.

John Marshall's papers show this theory in practice. In 1837, for instance, he bought larch, elm and beech plants for planting in Lanthwaite Wood, but he clearly also had a substantial proportion of fir trees there; in a letter of 1841 to his agent, suggesting that the wood had been neglected, he says: 'I think a plantation of evergreen very desirable'. The word 'plantation' is significant as it suggested woodland planted where there was none before.

In 1838, John Marshall sold 2014 larch trees from Loweswater Holme at 6½ pence a tree. The Holme was probably a timber wood. Lanthwaite, on the other hand, was clearly coppiced and was the haunt of bark peelers. Oak bark was peeled from the poles and sold to tanners (such as Joseph Iredell of Red Howe) for use in the processing of skins. A ton of oak bark from Lanthwaite was valued at £2 10/- in 1838. It must have been of high quality; in 1840, a ton of bark was valued at only 6 shillings and 10 pence, and a ton of large bark at two shillings.

It is usual to suggest that the amount of woodland in the British countryside has diminished greatly in the last century or so. Certainly the wars took their toll and B. L. Thompson in his book 'The Lake District and the National Trust' (1946) lists a number of woods in Loweswater which were cut down during both World Wars. A comparison of a modern ordnance survey map with its equivalent of a century ago, however, shows only very small differences in the shape of woodland in the parish. The main difference seems to be in the manner of their management, not in their extent.

THE REWARDS OF INDUSTRY[1]

Beware the name that has too obvious an explanation. 'Oak Bank' for instance. What is more natural than to look for a stand of oak trees nearby? But Mr Bolton of Lorton (in a lecture of 1891) had another suggestion. He cites evidence of an old trade that used to be carried out on the western bank of the Cocker. 'The late Mr Iredale of Red Howe had found the old tan pits used at this place, and Mr Bell (of Latterhead) told me that while he was making a sheep dipping place in a portion of his Orchard, they dug into a tan pit, with bark still in and in very good preservation. The sides of the pit were boarded and he has a portion which he took out - firm and strong as heart of oak. From this it would appear that a thriving industry had been carried on here and the name Oak Bank probably points to an origin of the trade.'

Mr Bolton could not put a date to the tan pit, only pointing out that the orchard's plum trees, which obviously succeeded it, were of a great age. There is plenty of evidence to show, however, that bark peeling, an industry essential to tanning, was in operation in the valley in the 1830s and 1840s.

Only oak bark yielded the tannin used in the production of high-quality leathers. In April and May, as the sap rose, the oak would be cut and a special knife used to strip the bark. After drying in the open, the bark was ground and layered in pits between the hides to be tanned.

One of the woods in Loweswater used as a source of oak bark was Lanthwaite Wood, which in the 1830s belonged to the Lord of the Manor, John Marshall.[2] Every year he ordered the wood to be coppiced - about seven tons of wood would produce about one ton of bark. In 1838, for instance, he paid a number of bark peelers, including Joseph Bank, about £27 for producing seven and a half tons of wood which he sold for £2 10/- a ton - a deal which hardly seems to make economic sense unless the value of the bark was extra. More significantly, in 1840, John Marshall bought nearly 14 tons of oak bark at £6 10/- a ton (a total of £88 -3-6) from John Fisher junior. The Fisher family were the owners of Cold Keld and Oak Bank, at least for the next ten years - John Fisher was in the process of going bankrupt.

Oak Bank itself consisted of about 50 acres between the River Cocker and the thin strip of land at the bottom of Low Fell farmed by Pottergill. Until the Fishers went bankrupt and had to sell, a few fields in

---

[1] First published February/March 1991.

[2] Lanthwaite Wood was in Brackenthwaite and John Marshall's manor of Loweswater did not extend to that side of the Cocker or Crummock, though he did receive some customary rents from Brackenthwaite. However he did purchase Scale Hill with Lanthwaite Wood in 1824, took the wood in hand and extended it onto land called 'The Waste'. Ed

the immediate vicinity of the houses were reserved for the use of the occupants of Cold Keld but after the sale - sometime in the early 1840s - all the land went to Oak Bank, Cold Keld being left merely with a barn and gardens. Oak Bank was then farmed by a succession of tenant farmers, usually labourers whose families show evidence of their wandering life. William Todd, for instance, who lived at Oak Bank in the 1850s, had been born in Whitehaven, had probably met his wife in Ennerdale, and their two children, Ann and Jackson, had been born in Loweswater.

Joseph Westray, Oak Bank's tenant in the late 1850s and early 1860s, was an Embleton man and his wife Margaret had been born in Bolton. They'd married in St John's in the Vale, one month after the birth of their eldest daughter, Betty. Their other children (Jane, aged 17, Joseph 14 and John 10) had all been born in Crosthwaite parish. In February 1882, Betty herself gave birth to an illegitimate daughter, Frances, in Loweswater.

Joseph and Margaret must have come to Loweswater in their late 30s or early 40s. In October 1862, when Joseph was 46, their stay at Oak Bank ended badly, under a distress for rent arrears. On Wednesday, 29th October, a sale was held at the house of almost all the Westrays' worldly belongings - a sale which gives a glimpse into the domestic life of a Victorian farming family.

According to the poster advertising the sale, the Westrays had three milch cows, three young bullocks, three young heifers, one chestnut horse, one bay mare, a pig and sow, four geese and a number of hens, chickens and other poultry. The notebook kept by John Thwaite, the auctioneer, is not always easy to match with the poster, but it does record that the chestnut horse was sold for £2 4/-, the four geese for six shillings each, a black cow for £8 16/-, a red cow for £7 10/-, and a red and white cow for £6 12/-. A calf went for £2 8/-. For some reason, no one wanted to buy the mare.

Crops were advertised for sale too - 'about Half an Acre of Wheat in Barn, about five Acres of Oats, 36 Stooks of Barley and a quantity of Meadow and Lee Hay in the Barn; about One Acre of Turnips and One ditto of Potatoes'. The turnips, 'to be eaten off', went for £1 5/-, the potatoes, in various 'stitches', went for a total of £1 12s 6d. 60 stooks of hay were sold at 3d, 3¼d or 3½d each, barley at 1/8d per stook, black oats at 1/6d. white oats at 1/4d and wheat at 2/4d.

Farming implements there were in plenty - a fork and rake (sold together for 8d), a muck fork (2/-), drags (2/-), hoes (8d), a hay fork and slasher (2/-). Weights and scales, tubs, threaptrees, sheepstools, a cheesepress, a saw, a scuttle, cart harness, cart stays, a cart saddle and collar, cart ropes, scythes, sacks, measures, stepladders, butter bowls, milk tips, a churn - all were sold for amounts varying between 9/6d (for the cart stays) and 3d (for a bottle).

Most poignant, however, is the list of 'Articles of Household Use' – the furniture which the family used every day 'comprising a good Clock and Case, Chairs, Mahogany and other Tables, Easy Chair ... Beds, Bedding, Wash Stand, Dressing-table, Looking Glasses ...' A feather bed fetched £2, a book case 6/-, a mirror 5/-. The Auctioneer's list reveals that the Westrays had eleven chairs in the house, two pictures (nature unspecified), a mahogany table, two feather beds, and an oak chest in addition to the book case and clock, hardly spartan living conditions. After the sale of course, they had nothing – and so far it's been impossible to trace where they went.

Loweswater smithy in the 1920s

IRON IN THEM THARE HILLS[1]

On 12th July 1871, Whitehaven Mines Ltd. issued a prospectus designed to attract subscribers to its latest venture. 'The properties to be acquired and developed by this company,' the prospectus said ' are ... the Floutern Tarn, Starling Dodd and Red Pike mines situated ... about midway between Ennerdale and Buttermere lakes.' If the ambitious scheme had gone ahead, the Loweswater valley could have been changed beyond all recognition.

The mineral the company was planning to develop was iron. Veins of ore could be traced on the surface in nine places, from just east of Floutern Tarn, to Scale Force and along Mosedale Beck, over an area of 6000 acres. There were two different types of ore, pudding ore (which sold at the time for 18 shillings to 20 shillings a ton) and blast ore (selling at 13 shillings to 16 shillings a ton). The Directors of the Company estimated that 100,000 to 120,000 tons of ore could be raised each year. In fact, the prospectus said confidently, the amount of ore in the ground was 'practically inexhaustible'.

Prospectuses are notoriously optimistic, of course, but any would-be investor would have been reassured to read the special report (on 23 October 1871) of Mr George Henwood, M. E., who had been employed to survey the land. His enthusiasm was enormous. 'There will be no great outlay in getting the material,' he said, 'and there is no limit to the quantity that may be raised ... I found this to be one of the great champion veins of the district'. He repeated the prediction of 'inexhaustible' veins and added: 'I can have no hesitation whatever in (saying) the development ... will add materially to the prosperity of the country and the pockets of the proprietors'. Just what everyone wanted to hear.

Naturally, arrangements had to be made for the accommodation of the miners. When the lead mine near the Netherclose road had opened in the 1830s, there had been a large increase in population in the valley with miners coming from as far away as Redruth. Mr Henwood proposed that accommodation should be provided either in the shape of a well-arranged comfortable barracks or cheap cottages which should be erected with a view to permanence and the comfort of the men and their families, in order to induce them to settle and remain at the mines. 'You by this means secure a permanent staff so essential to the regular and successful conduct of mining operations.' These cottages would probably have been built in Loweswater itself.

In conclusion, Mr Henwood said, the directors possessed 'a property of great magnitude, from which immense profits will be realised' and added modestly, 'I have discovered immense deposits of iron ore and other minerals in all parts of the world, particularly in India'.

---

[1] First published July 1986.

Over the next two years some small trials were made to test the quality and extent of the ore, the main trials being on Gale Fell and at a point about 30 yards to the east of the foot of Scale Force. Following these trials, on 30 October 1873, Mr John A Dixon of King Street, Whitehaven, was asked to inspect the sites and make a further report on them. What followed, on 19 November, was a blow to Mr Henwood's reputation as the finder of 'immense deposits'.

Mr Dixon inspected all nine sites and his report must have made depressing reading for the Directors and investors in the Company. The same phrases crop up again and again. 'There is nothing here that would warrant any outlay of capital.' 'A few tons of ore of fair quality ... little or no ore...' 'This drift has yielded from 40 -50 tons.' A far cry from the 120,000 tons per annum predicted by the optimistic prospectus.

From his inspection of the sites, Mr Dixon concluded that to continue mining operations would prove extremely costly, for a wide variety of reasons: 'the isolated position of these fells for getting and engaging miners, the difficulty in reaching the higher levels and the getting of materials, timber and tools to the place and the transit of the ore from the several drift mouths in the steep irregular mountain sides to the railway when made ... not forgetting the cost of making a railway ... I cannot recommend you invest any large amount of capital further developing this property'.

Mr Dixon's report cannot have pleased his employers but it was a blessing in disguise for the Loweswater valley, on account of the railway which would have had to be built to transport the ore. There were two alternative routes proposed for this railway. The first was for a double line with 2 foot gauge running from the Knockmurton Mines, across Crossdale Beck and Gavel Fell to Floutern Tarn; this would have cost about £20,000, a large sum indeed. The second route, however, as even Mr Dixon acknowledged, would have been far better. This would have comprised a 4 foot 8 inch gauge railway running from Cockermouth through the Vale of Lorton past Scale Hill Hotel and up the Mosedale Beck valley - about 11 miles of track. The only drawback to this excellent idea was that it was even more expensive than the first proposed route, £130,000.

With the collapse of hopes for the mines, of course, the railway scheme came to nothing. If it had been implemented, Loweswater might now resemble one of those once-so-green Welsh valleys.

NOTICE IS HEREBY GIVEN,

That proper Persons have been appointed by JOHN MARSHALL, Esq.

TO WATCH AND PROTECT THE

TROUT

And other Fish,

During the Spawning Season, from being taken or destroyed in the Lakes of Crummock, Buttermere, and Loweswater, or in the Brooks or Streams communicating therewith; and if any Person or Persons shall be found attempting to take, kill, or destroy, any Trout or other Fish, or any of the Spawn or Fry, within his Manor of Loweswater, he or they will be prosecuted as the Law directs.

LOWESWATER, 21st OCTOBER, 1839.

T. BAILEY & SON, PRINTERS, COCKERMOUTH.

A notice protecting trout, 1839 -
by permission of Waugh & Musgrave, Solicitors

ON THE HOOK[1]

Fishing has been going on ever since people and fish have been in the same world together. The inhabitants of the Iron Age settlement on the lower slopes of Grasmoor may have fished Crummock Water; the Norsemen living between Scale Force and the lake certainly will have. For these early inhabitants of the valley, fish provided a nutritious supplement to a sometimes dull diet.

The earliest references to organised fishing in the parish are in Percy papers. The Earls of Northumberland owned Loweswater and the surrounding manors in the two or three centuries before the Tudors. Not that they thought much of the agricultural value of the area; the Percy Great Survey of 1507 reports of Cumberland that:

> *The country is very cold, hard and barren for the winter ... their greatest gain consisteth in breeding of cattle ... ; because the greatest part of the country consists in wastes and mountains they have little tillage.*

The Percys made the most of what they had by renting out the fisheries of lakes and rivers in their manors and their papers preserve the rental costs. In 1439 for instance, the fishery rental of Loweswater lake was two shillings per annum and for Mockerkin Tarn (then known as Ternemaryn), one shilling. Buttermere cost 6s. 3d. By far the most expensive place to fish (and therefore no doubt the most profitable) was Crummock Water, costing 26/8d, later raised to 33/4d with a further one shilling for an 'elyng'. Eels were evidently plentiful in those days; there was also an elegarth in Brackenthwaite, near the River Cocker. In addition, some repairs had been undertaken on the river between Loweswater and Crummock, and it cost one shilling to fish this 'new stream'. Forty or so years later, prices had hardly altered; Buttermere in 1483 cost the same, Loweswater and Mockerkin Tarn had been lumped together with Mosedale Beck for 2/6d and Crummock fishery rental had actually gone down by three shillings.[2]

Then, as always, there were poachers. In 1457, John Jackson of Millhill was fined 4d for 'fishing with a net' and a year later William Harrison was fined for catching trout. According to Bouch, the chief method of fishing was with a hook and net but, upstream, coops were often used. These had to be arranged so that there was a gap in the centre of the stream wide enough 'for a sow and her five little pigs'.

---

[1] First published October/November 1989.

[2] Prices taken from Bouch, 1948.

Three centuries later, in 1766, the Court Rolls which recorded the offences of John Jackson and William Harrison were still naming poachers. Joseph Richardson, Jonathan Burnyeat and William Rothery were fined twenty shillings each for 'fishing in Church Beck in the night-time'. They all paid the fine the same day it was imposed which suggests that their activities may well have been profitable on other nights.

In 1794, William Hutchinson in his 'History and Antiquities of Cumberland' records pike, trout, bass and eels in Loweswater and the same in Crummock, with the addition of char.[1] Early in the next century, poachers of this plenty were still causing problems for another Lord of the Manor, John Marshall. In October 1838, he wrote to his agent, Richard Atkinson, to say that something had to be done and suggested that hand bills be spread around the village; he complained that the punishment for poaching was too small. A week later he was changing his mind. 'If you have not got any hand bills printed, it may be sufficient to put up a written notice, in the Blacksmith's shop and Church and School, that offenders will certainly be prosecuted.' A committee against poaching had been formed at Cockermouth, and Marshall said firmly: 'I'll spare no expense to stop it' (the poaching). In the end he was called upon to pay out ten shilling each now and again to John and Richard Clerk for 'watching fish in the night' with no indication of any great success.

The 'licensed' fisherman of the time, who paid Marshall £5 for a year's fishery rent, was Robert Jopson; he paid an extra ten shillings per year for renting a boat. (Unfortunately for Marshall's accounts, he himself had to pay Major General Henry Wyndham £8 8 shillings so he could take his friends fishing on Crummock.) In 1851, the census records as 'char and trout fisher' (presumably working on Crummock) John Tyson from Gillerthwaite. Aged 68, he shared a house with his wife, Mary, his daughter Mary and her husband, William Simon (a farm labourer) and their daughter, also Mary, aged 8 months. Gillerthwaite was one of the busiest corners of the parish. Joseph's son, Isaac (aged 38) carried on a cartwright's business there and of course there was the blacksmith's shop by the road, worked by Robert Beck.

Thirty years later, at much the same age as his father, Isaac Tyson had progressed from being a cartwright to being a joiner to renting the fishery. By this time his first wife had died and he had married again and had a teenage daughter – unsurprisingly she was called Mary.

By this time, tourism was increasing in importance for the local economy. A number of farmers were supplementing their agricultural

---

[1] He also records what seems to be a gamehunter's paradise, with 'grouse, hares and partridges. Many wild duck on the lakes in winter. On the fells, marts, foxes and wild cats. About six years ago were red deer on the hills, which had probably bred there for ages'.

earnings by taking in visitors. Thomas Edmondson of Godferhead let out a furnished house during the summer months and Joseph Beck, the blacksmith son of Robert, owned and let out Kirkhead House 'whole or part, with or without attendance'. Mrs Sarah Statter of Low Park rented out 'apartments' at High Cross: 'Visitors will receive every attention with moderate terms'. Advertisements for all three owners stressed fishing - for sport - as one of the attractions of the area.

The visitor who stayed at Scale Hill could, of course, enjoy the fruits of other people's fishing labours (and even pass them off as their own?) in the hotel's famous potted char. The proprietor offered 'fishing boats and experienced fishermen' to his residents. In Buttermere, the owners of the Victoria and Fish Hotels had a more modern, more aggressive sales approach. In Jenkinson's 'Guide to the English Lakes', (published in 1876) the Victoria is described by the proprietess, Grace Edmondson, as 'a most desirable Residence for parties fond of Angling, which may be enjoyed to repletion, the Lakes and Streams abounding with Trout and Char. Fishing parties may confidently rely upon meeting with every attention; the promotion of whose comfort will ever be the study of the proprietess'. The hotel boasted 'a large and commodious Coffee-room, spacious Sitting-rooms, Smoking-rooms, well-ventilated Bedrooms' - like Mrs Statter's apartments at High Cross which had 'every comfort combined with Moderate charges ... fitted up and replete with every modern improvement appertaining to a first class hotel'. Jane Ann Clark describes her Fish Hotel in almost identical terms, the only differences between the two hotels appearing to be that the Fish's rooms were airy as well as well-ventilated and Mrs Clark served lunch from 1 pm until 3, whereas the Victoria stopped serving at 4.

In the text of the guidebook, Henry Irwin Jenkinson provides further valuable information for his angling readers. Buttermere and Crummock, he says, both contain char and trout, and a boat and boatman can be hired for a day's fishing for five shillings. For the boatmen who ran this service, however, fishing was only a part and not the largest part of their business. More profitable were the coach parties of tourists from Keswick who had three hours' spare time in Buttermere. Jenkinson recommends a visit to Scale Force but advises against the 'stony path', in favour of a boat trip. For one shilling a boatman would row you to the waterfall and back; the boat had to be shared of course, with five other people if it was a small boat, with nine it is was large. Privacy could only be ensured for 1/6d for which the boatman would come with you to the force, if required. Alternatively, if the visitor was not fond of waterfalls, a trip from one end of Crummock to the other was five shillings (or six shillings if the waterfall was to be included as well). The boatmen clearly would undertake any trip that seemed as if it might be profitable; however, as Jenkinson points out, 'during the busy part of the season there is often difficulty in obtaining a boat without delay'. For some visitors, hurrying to cram everything into the three hours before the coach left again, it had to be the 'stony path' after all.

Fishing in one form or another, including poaching, has always been a part of life in Loweswater but for the residents it was always a sideline, a subsidiary occupation. It was a full-time job only for the elderly, when they had given up their farms to younger more able-bodied men. Like tailoring and shoemaking and butchering, and tourism, it was something to turn to in times of hardship when agriculture for one reason or another could not fully support the family. Not for them a lazy day's angling for pleasure; fishing was always a serious business.

The Loweswater and Brackenthwaite centenary show, 1972 – photo L&DFLHS archive

Chapter 3: COMMUNITY AND CULTURE

The further you go back, the more the people of Loweswater had responsibility for their own lives and the more their survival as a community depended on co-operation. These articles address the various ways in which the people of Loweswater worked together, through necessity or choice and at work or play, and in other ways developed or maintained a culture which bound them together. The origins of Loweswater are not recorded, but the landscape still shows the remains of open arable fields of Anglian character next to Crummock. As in Lorton, Buttermere and Embleton, strips of land were once allocated to tenants for their staple oats, but were ploughed and harvested communally. They worked together or died together, and had to control the population to match the resources that their land provided, in an ecological balance.

Apart from producing food, a shared religious belief and practice was the bedrock of community cohesion, and *No paint or sham* addresses the church as a building which was built and maintained by the community. The clergy, appointed from outside to both serve and supervise, are covered under Lordship and Authority. Effective communities need conformity, and throughout these articles Quakers appear as different. In Loweswater they grew in number to become in some ways a separate commununuity with their own chapter in this book . *Making a way* reminds us that Loweswater was responsible for its own highways until 1889. The County maintained only Deepa (Scale) Bridge; the tourists and the carriers on the Whitehaven to Keswick road paid nothing.

Education for most children was of little concern until the late eighteenth century, and in the 1830s a Bill to provide universal education failed because the Church of England was to control it. A curate's school had operated in Loweswater since 1782, but John Marshall's village school of 1839, the subject of several articles in this chapter, was part philanthropy but also a deliberate removal of the control of the established Church. The Quakers must have approved.

Perhaps missing from this series is an article on the poor, though they are present within several articles. The Loweswater records are thin, and soon after the New Poor Law of 1834 the poor of the township were accommodated in the Cockermouth Union workhouse at Loweswater's expense. But there were very few from agricultural districts.

Pastime with good company and *On the fiddle* describe the community at play, in which we can see the residue of long established customs and traditions, but only the ones which people wished or needed to keep.

NO PAINT OR SHAM[1]

In 1827, the inhabitants of Loweswater applied to the Bishop of Chester - in whose diocese the parish then was - for permission to build a new chapel, 'the chapel of Loweswater aforesaid having been in such a ruinous and decayed state that Divine Service could not safely be performed therein'.

There was certainly a chapel in Loweswater from the fourteenth century onwards but the first references to what we can (fairly) confidently say was the building pulled down in 1827 dated from the end of the seventeenth century.[2] There is a brief reference in 1683 in Quaker records to 'repairs to the bell-house' and then a more detailed account of the building in 1695. From time to time parishioners were required to answer a questionnaire from the Bishop concerning the state of their church or chapel, and the 1695 and 1700 answers - almost identical - survive in the Cumbria Record Office.

Unfortunately, the questions and therefore the answers, were not much interested in the appearance of the building. Regarding the exterior for instance, the parishioners simply say: 'Our Chappel is in good and Sufficient Repair both for the Roof, Windows, Floor and Sets'. However, it is possible to gleam information from the answers about the interior furnishings and a little about the kind of services held in the chapel.

'We have a font of stone and a cover in our Chappell, our curate baptises publicly in ye Font.' The communion Table had a decent 'carpet'(by which they meant a covering for everyday use) and 'another covering of white Linnen to be spread thereon at ye time of Administration of ye Lords Supper'. Holy Communion was supposed to be celebrated three times yearly but the parishioners merely report that the curate 'causes ye Lords Supper to be celebrated yearly'. For this he wore a 'decent surplice ... with such other Habit as is suitable in his office' and used 'a communion cup with a cover and a pewter Flagon'.

The curate did not have much to complain about at Loweswater. He had 'a convenient seat wherein to read Divine Service (and) a Pulpit with a decent cushion'. {Did he preach sitting down?) He also had all the necessary books: 'a large Bible of the last Translation, a Booke of Common Prayer, published Ano 1662, a Book of Homilies, a printed Table of degrees' (showing the degrees of relationship within which relatives could not marry) and 'a Booke of Cannons' (church law). These books, together with the parchment register books, the Churchwardens' account books and the 'decent surplice' were kept in 'a strong chest, well lockt'.

---

[1] First published October/November 1990.

[2] We know that there was a chapel in 1125 when it was given to the Priory of St Bees, See *As Clerkes Finder Written*. The chapel was raised to parish status and its church yard consecrated by Archbishop Wickwane of York in 1281. See Wilson, 1915. Ed.

In 1700 a belfry was built onto the church by John Bowman of Ullock. The money necessary for this work was raised by the overseers of the work, John Allason of Godferhead and John Tolson (probably of High Nook). A church rate was levied though the parish's many Quakers refused to pay, as indeed they had refused to pay for the previous repairs in 1683. John Allason for one must have regretted the days before the Toleration Act of 1689 when he could confiscate property in lieu of unpaid rates. '1683', say Quaker records, ' the 20th day of 12th month [February] came John Allason of Grafred [Godferhead] and took away from Anne Dixon of Waterend a pair of leather mittens worth 7d for 6d demanded for repair of the bell-house'. (There were about 80 households in the parish, so if each was required to pay 6d for the repairs the approximate cost would have been 40/- or £2.)

In 1707, a new curate came to the parish, Henry Forrest, who, with his wife Ellinor, was to stay for 34 years. Records for this time are scarce and the only work on the church that we know about is the planting of sycamores in the churchyard on 16th February 1710/11.[1] No doubt maintenance and minor repairs were carried out whenever necessary.

Henry and Ellinor Forrest died within five days of each other in March 1741/2 and the new curate, Joseph Wilkinson, survived only six months after his appointment. Then, in 1742, came along Thomas Cowper who has been mentioned in these articles several times before.

It is clear, from notes that Thomas made in the parish registers, that the church had been neglected and could not longer be described as 'in good and Sufficient Repair'. In 1751, Thomas records major works: 'N.B. The roof was taken off ye body of Loweswater church and ye South side was first slated with Ewecragg Slate'. Two years later, the chancel roof was also replaced and re-slated 'at which time also a great part of ye Church was plastered'.

In 1778, the church was 'flagged and paved' so the flooring before this may have been either bare earth or cobbles. About this time, too, the decision was taken to stop teaching the boys of the parish in the church - a habit which had survived since the Middle Ages. For some reason, Thomas, or his parishioners, decided that 'it is not fit to teaching in the church', and in 1780, a schoolhouse was built - the building that is now Rose Cottage at the bottom of Vicarage Hill. By this time, Thomas was saying Holy Communion between eight and twelve times a year.

The yard in which the chapel stood was very small as only relatively recently had burials taken place at Loweswater rather than at the mother church of St Bees. The answers of 1695 refer to it as being 'adequately fenced'; coincidentally, the old surviving gravestone - that of

---

[1] Mentioned in parish registers.

Isabella Tolson of High Nook and her ten month old daughter – dates from the same year.

The most detailed account of the church, however, dates from 1891. Or rather from both 1810 and 1891. In the latter year, John Bolton of Lorton quizzed his mother-in-law, Mrs Lancaster, formerly Miss Iredell of Loweswater, about her childhood memories of the area. (Allowances must be made of course for the vagaries of memory – Mrs Lancaster occasionally mixed up dates and fathers and sons.) 'Mrs Lancaster,' said Mr Bolton, 'describes the old chapel as having a porch on the Kirkgate side and just inside the church was the old font. It was here that the bellringer stood. She thinks that there was only one bell and that not a good one. The stairs sprang from beside the font and the gallery extended along the west gable supported by pillars.'

(Mr Bolton adds that he had 'heard' – he does not give his source – that the pupils used to be taught beside the pillars.)

'There were pews on each side of the aisle, large, roomy, high-backed oak pews. There was an arch dividing the nave or body of the Church from the Chancel and it was against this arch on the left-hand side – looking towards the Chancel – that the Pulpit stood.'

'The pulpit for the priest and the one for the clerk were also of oak – there was no paint or sham about the place – good, old, self-coloured oak. There was a reading desk close to the pulpit, one stop or so up from the floor – the clerk's laal cabin as she [Mrs Lancaster] calls it, was on the ground floor.'

The richer families of the parish – the families from Foulsyke, Miresyke, High Cross and so on – had their 'ancestral pews' in the choir, known locally as 't'wheer'. 'The windows were long and very narrow and arched and filled with leaded lights.' There was no organ – Mrs Lancaster remembered a square pitch pipe, long since lost. Nor were hymns sung, but only metrical psalms.

'The clerk was not an old man,' remembered Mrs Lancaster. 'He was John Jackson of Bar Yeat. Before the psalm ... John used to march down the church aisle and up to the Gallery and give the Psalm out, the Congregation turning their backs on the Priest to face the singers. Loweswater singers were considered good ones.'

This statement is also witnessed to by Thomas Cowper who in 1757 had written a verse in the register in memory of Anne Bank of Low Park 'a charming singer of psalms' who died on October 20th that year aged 33. 'Sweet Harmonist,' he called her and pictured her '...in concert with th'angelic choir (giving) all glory to the Lamb while listening Saints admire'.

Alas, by 1827, the church that Thomas Cowper, Anne Bank and Mrs Lancaster had worshipped in was 'ruinous'. There is a story that it was the victim of a fire from which most moveable objects had fortunately been saved. It was demolished and on 25th August 1829, the new chapel was consecrated 'upon the site of the old Chapel ... finished, furnished and adorned ... with all necessaries for Divine Worship'.

A NOTE ON DATES

Until 1752, the year started on March 25th; the preceding three months were considered to be in the previous year. Thus, the churchyard sycamores were planted on the 16th February of what they called 1710 but what we'd nowadays consider to be 1711. This kind of date is generally written as 1710/11 to show both the recorded and the modern date.

Loweswater Church with evening shadows

MAKING WAY[1]

The first roads in Loweswater were prehistoric, tracks lying high up on the fells rather than in the valleys which were nasty swampish places where unpleasant things like wolves and wild boar lurked. It is possible that prehistoric man used Coledale Pass which would be close to his settlement on the lower slopes of Grasmoor.

Even as late as the Middle Ages, tracks like these would be simply worn down by constant use and would require no maintenance. In the later Middle Ages however, travel became more common. People from Loweswater made their way more frequently to market at Cockermouth or to the mills at Brackenthwaite and Lorton. Carts were few, travel generally being on foot or by horse or even sled, but, even so, roads would need to be kept in a reasonable state, not too narrow, and free from natural hazards like fallen trees or overflowing streams.

Though there were no laws assigning responsibility in this matter, farmers were expected to maintain any roads that crossed their lands, whether they were scarcely-used local tracks or heavily-frequented major routes; in practice many farmers failed to do anything or were positively obstructive.

In 1523, for instance, the Manor Court Rolls record that Peter Thomson and John Bank were fined for 'narrowing the highway in the territory of Brackenthwaite to the common nuisance'. Three years later, they still had not put the problem right and the road had what the Rolls politely term 'defects', which probably means it was full of potholes.

Roads were gated; gates divided each farm from its neighbours and field from field - there was also a gate leading from the cultivated land out onto the common. These gates frequently fell into disrepair. In 1520, for instance, Jenkyn Fletcher was cited for 'not keeping up of one gate on the highway which leads between Eggermont and Keswick and also between Loweswater and Cockermouth to the common nuisance of the Lord's tenants there'.

All these offences were presented to the court by the inhabitants of the manor, by the men who were personally inconvenienced by any neglect. Keeping such gates in repair, however, was clearly considered at least by some people as an imposition as witness the case of Robert Hudson and his wife in 1525; when they wanted to complain against a decision of the Lord, their defiant response was to 'cut down their gate upon the highway upon the gateposts'. For 'carrying the same gate into the water called Crombokwatter', they were fined twenty shillings.

When Mary Tudor put her mind to the problems of the Kingdom's roads in 1555, she ordained that two surveyors were to be appointed by

[1] First published December 1989-January 1990.

each parish to enquire into the state of roads and bridges. Every parishioner with land worth £50 or more was required to provide material, tools and six days' labour for repairs if necessary. Mary cannot have known much about places like Loweswater; even two hundred years later most 'estates' in the parish were worth only between £20 and £40 a year, and only two or three were worth £300 a year. The value of these estates in Mary's time would have been extremely small except, of course, for the estate of the Lord of the Manor.

This lack of resources would inevitably have caused problems and the act was in any case badly enforced throughout the country. Judging by the Manor Court Rolls, individual farmers were still considered responsible for roads crossing their lands and still continued to be negligent from time to time. In 1723, Ann Skelton, John Harrison and William Pearson were ordered jointly to repair a gate at the edge of Watergate land. Nearly 30 years later, John's son (another John) and William's son, Peter, and his wife were being told off for not repairing High Nook Bridge. (They were given six months to carry out the repairs or be fined thirteen shillings.) Other offenders were Joseph Skelton who in 1756 was ordered to repair the 'hiway on the south side of Stockbridge leading from the said Lords Mill' and Ruther Fletcher who in 1786 ploughed up a footway in a 'certain field called the Croft leading to the Marcut towns of Whitehaven and Cockermouth'.

Disputes over access sometimes occurred. In 1743, John Iredale of Thackthwaite and Joseph Beaty clashed over whether Joseph had right of access over John's land. The court decided that he had, and ordered John to 'make the way sufficient ... for cart and carriage'. In 1784, there arose the complicated issue of which way Pottergill, at the foot of Low Fell, should be approached. John Grainger was brought to court by the Lord's bailiff, John Fisher of Cold Keld, for making a track from Foulsyke. The court decided that the correct approach was from Latterhead and fined John Grainger three shillings and sixpence.

In 1836, a new Highways Act was passed by one of William IV's parliaments. Every rated inhabitant of the parish had now to attend a vestry meeting on or within 14 days of 25 March, to choose two Surveyors of Highways. The qualification for being a surveyor was ownership of an estate (either in your own right or in your wife's) to the value of £10 per annum or personal property to the value of £100 or the occupation (resident in the parish or in an adjoining one) of property worth £25 per annum. This included a much wider range of people; in 1855, for instance, John Simon of Park and Joseph Mitchinson of Oak Bank, both farmers, were surveyors for the ensuing year.

The duties of a surveyor were, of course, to keep an eye on the state of highways in the parish and to put in train necessary repairs, with the help of a parish rate. At the end of the year of office, accounts had to be presented together with a report as to the state of all 'roads, bridges, hedges, ditches and watercourses' and of all 'nuisances and encroachments on the road', also what repairs had been undertaken, how much they had cost and the amount of rate that had been levied to pay for them. John Marshall, Lord of the Manor, grumbled that in 1842, he paid £6 18s in highway rates in Loweswater and it is unlikely he was getting tarmaced roads for his money.

As a result of the poor quality of roads there were inevitably a number of accidents, some fatal. Coroners' reports record the deaths of Ann Wells who in 1820 fell from her horse on the road in Brackenthwaite, and of Hannah Salkeld (aged 18) who fell from a cart on the Loweswater-Whinfell road in 1852. John Fisher of Cold Keld was another victim of a road accident, though his death resulted from a fall from his horse near Ouse Bridge, Bassenthwaite. In 1908, another unhappy accident on the Buttermere road near Hassness resulted in the death of John Jackson aged 21 who was fatally injured when he was thrown from a cart after a collision with a motor car. By that time, however, after 1889, care for local roads had passed out of parish hands into the control of the newly formed County Council.

EXAM TIME[1]

On 17 May 1872, Her Majesty's Inspector for Schools, Mr. F. R. Sandford, visited Loweswater to inspect the school as he was required to do under the 1870 Education Act. His report, sent to the vicar, the Rev. George M. Tandy, was full of half-praise: the children's handwriting was 'pretty good', their reading 'fairly correct', their spelling and arithmetic 'pretty fair'. He recommended more sewing and less knitting, and commended the geography teaching but pointed out that 'attentions should be given primarily to perfecting the elementary subjects'.

One of the school's problems was that there was no properly qualified teacher. The only teacher was George White, a young man who was uncertificated. The Inspector had clearly had a talk with young Mr White and enclosed, in the letter to the vicar, a special form for the teacher. Form XXXI was entitled 'Syllabus for Male Candidates' and laid down the syllabus for examinations to be held in December 1872 for candidate teachers. In his rooms over the school, George White must have pored over this syllabus with some trepidation. It was designed for student teachers but teachers already in the job could also take the examination, entering for either first or second year papers as they chose.

From the syllabus, George White would have seen that there were certain subjects which were compulsory – if he failed any of these, he would not get his Certificate. The compulsory subjects were reading, spelling, penmanship, school management, composition and arithmetic. In addition, he could – if he wished – take grammar, geography, history, geometry, economy, music and drawing. In almost all the subjects, the second year was generally the same as the first but marked more rigorously.

As far as marking was concerned, there were five categories: excellent, good, fair, moderate, and imperfect. All of these could earn the candidate a pass; below 'imperfect' was only 'fail'.

For the examination in reading, George White had to read aloud 'with distinct utterance, due attention to the punctuation and just expression'. Whichever year he opted for, he had to learn by heart at least three hundred lines of poetry or two hundred of prose and be ready to repeat some of it at the exam. The Education Department was keen on rote learning; another circular (in 1878) told teachers to 'call attention to the value of learning by heart ... as a means of storing the children's memories with noble and elevated sentiments'.

George White may well have dropped a few marks on this particular exam. Two years later, the inspector felt compelled to comment on the Loweswater children's sloppy pronunciation, and remarked: 'The Master should be careful himself to enunciate distinctly in giving reading

---

[1] First published March 1994

and dictation lessons.' It was a problem on which the inspector was to comment frequently; the real problem may simply have been that George White shared his pupils' Cumbrian accent and the inspector disapproved.

Penmanship was largely judged by the standard of writing in the various examination papers. The examiners preferred the handwriting which was generally practised in the earlier part and middle of the last century, which was far better than that now in common use. Writing ... is apt to be too small and indistinct'. George White can have had few problems here; surviving examples of his writing, chiefly on receipts addressed to the vicar, show his writing to be large and elegant with one or two flourishes, very easy to read.

'School Management' involved answering questions on the best methods of teaching various subjects, on how to timetable lessons and keep registers. The candidates also had to teach a class in front of the examiners and answer questions on matters of 'moral discipline'. George White certainly knew how to keep order in his school - the Inspector repeatedly commented on that fact and on the 'pleasant manners of the children' but he may in fact have been an intimidating teacher. In 1879, only seven years after White's examination, the Inspector commented that 'Good order is maintained but the Master should endeavour by a kindly and quiet manner to draw out the intelligence of his scholars and induce them to answer questions with freedom'.

Grammar and composition was a joint subject and rather taxing - the candidate had to be prepared to parse words from poetry by Gray or Dryden and to convert the verse into prose. He also had to write a composition on a subject of the examiner's choice. Grammar was never a particularly strong subject at Loweswater school but that may not have been George White's fault; the subject was probably not very high on the children's list of priorities.

Arithmetic, on the other hand, was always satisfactory at the school so George probably had no problem with the arithmetic exam which included mental and paper work and some algebra.

In addition to all this, George White may have taken geography and history exams; both these subjects were taught by him at Loweswater and taught to the Inspector's satisfaction. Unsurprisingly, both subjects tended to concentrate on a knowledge of Britain and the British Empire but candidates for the teacher's examination also had to be able to draw a map of the world and maps of every country in Europe, as well as answering questions on Scottish history before the Union. The list of special subjects for historical study seems unusually morbid, not just the Battles of Bosworth and Waterloo but also the deaths of Henry III and Queen Elizabeth.

Undoubtedly the oddest syllabus George White may have studied, however, was in 'economy' - no details of monetary theories or even of the virtues of saving and such like, but a first year syllabus that covered 'elementary questions in sanitary science'. Science was not included in the examination for teachers but candidates could claim extra marks for exams they had taken elsewhere which could cover such topics.

Music was included however; candidates had to be able to write down music in both treble and bass clefs, and to know both major and minor scales. The children had to learn songs by heart - four for the infants and at last eight for the older children. The younger children usually sang by ear, the older ones could sing by note too, although they had to know the songs by heart. The school benefited if the children could read music - a payment of 6d was made for each child singing by ear but one shilling if they could sing from music. The children's singing at Loweswater was usually described as 'satisfactory'.

On 20 March 1875, the Inspector sent George White's certificate to the Rev. George Tandy. George White had certainly passed, but only just. First division (or first class) candidates needed to acquire 575 marks or more. George White received a place in the 4th division, which means he achieved between 250 and 300 marks. He cannot have been displeased, however; it made his post at Loweswater secure and entitled him to a higher salary. He eventually retired from the school in July 1909, at a salary of £100 per annum having taught in Loweswater for 37 years.

Loweswater School, early twentieth century - as built by John Marshall in 1839. L&DFLHS archive

SCHOOL REPORTS[1]

George Mercer Tandy, vicar of Loweswater in the 1870s, cannot have looked forward to communications from the Education Department but his feelings were probably mild compared to the nervousness and anxiety with which George White, schoolmaster at Loweswater school, awaited the results of the school's annual inspection.

Her Majesty's Inspector of Schools, the Rev. C. H. Parez, who lived at Stanwix in Carlisle, had the task of seeing that the provisions of the 1870 Education Act were enforced in Cumberland, Westmorland and Furness Lancashire. His concert was to ensure that adequate schooling was provided for every child; this included not only ensuring a high standard of teaching but also the provision of suitable buildings.

Loweswater was fortunate in having a purpose-built school only forty years old, but from time to time Mr Parez's reports make it clear that the building was not perfect. Most of his remarks seem prompted by some specific event. In June 1878, he evidently found the schoolroom rather stuffy; he recommends: 'The room being low Tobin's ventilators would be found of use'. In 1884, he commented: 'It is desirable that a boarded floor should be made' although he does not specify what substance the present floor was made of. In 1875, the day of the inspection was apparently wet; he wrote: 'The roof drainage should be carried off more effectually'. It is probably unwise to speculate on what made him comment in 1879 that 'A urinal (with partitions) should be made'.

But, of course, Mr Claude M Parez was principally concerned with the standard of teaching in the schools he inspected and with the attainments and behaviour of the pupils. He was under no illusions as to the difficulties which schools and teachers faced. In his report for 1876, he quotes the case of the parish of Dearham where the population considered almost entirely of colliers. 'The first mistress of the girl's school was almost in desperation on entering into her duties in consequence of the rough habits and the bad language they (the girls) were accustomed to use.'

George White did not face quite such difficult problems; indeed, the school lists that for some years survive with Mr Parez's reports show that with the vast majority of his pupils he did not even have attendance problems. Moreover, once in school, he seems to have had no difficulty in controlling the children. Time and again, Claude Parez comments; 'The order is good' (1873), although he adds 'somewhat of a lack of smartness is apparent generally'. 'The order is excellent' (1874); 'the boys went through their school drill with commendable smartness' (1875); 'Good order prevails' (1876). Only once, in 1871, did any of George White's pupils disgrace him by copying during the examinations.

---

[1] First published in Aug/Sept 1990.

Unfortunately, when the question of attainment raises its head, Mr Parez's reports generally make depressing reading, such words as 'pretty fair' and 'moderate' being all too frequent. 'Creditable' is the strongest word Mr Parez uses.

The children, who numbered between 35 and 40 each year (5 or 6 being infants) were all examined in elementary subjects - reading, writing and arithmetic - and in grammar, needlework and geography. One or two of the older, and better, pupils took special subjects such as domestic economy, physical geography and botany. During the examinations the children had to recite passages and explain any difficult words in the passages; they took dictation to display their handwriting and spelling and they answered questions. They produced samples of needlework; the boys performed drill and everyone sang.

One of George White's biggest problems was the local accent which, to judge by Mr Parez's reports, may have caused more children to fail than any lack of reading ability. In the first report that survives (1872), Mr Parez describes the reading as 'fairly correct' but 'indistinct'. In 1877, he comments: 'The reading is very monotonous and wanting in expression; continued efforts should be made to obtain greater distinctness and articulation.' George White cannot have been pleased to read in 1874 that he himself should be careful to 'enunciate distinctly in giving Reading and Dictation lessons'. By 1881, however, he was winning the battle: 'The articulation is improved in distinctness but greater fluency is required'.

The children's handwriting was generally adjudged to be 'pretty good' although their ability to spell was usually the poor side of average. (George White's son, George junior, usually let his father down by failing writing examinations.) In 1886, Mr Parez went so far as to say 'The slate and paperwork show care and intelligence and deserve much credit'. The weakest subject by far was arithmetic; George White conducted a continual battle to raise the number of passes to a respectable level and year after year Mr Parez commented: 'The infants are backward in arithmetic'. 'The arithmetic of the three higher standards [is] below par.' 'The arithmetic is very moderate.'

George White certainly suffered from a lack of resources; Claude Parez comments on the lack of a blackboard, a ball-frame (probably an abacus) and various maps. However, it may well be that George White was part of his own problem. Mr Parez was concerned enough in 1873 to write: 'Good order is maintained but the Master should endeavour by a kindly and quiet manner to draw out the intelligence of his scholars and induce them to answer questions with freedom'. George White, it seems, was a little intimidating to his pupils.

Nevertheless, despite Claude Parez's reservations, examination results at Loweswater school never fell beneath an acceptable level. Even in 1877, when Mr Perez was at his most critical (describing spelling as 'very poor', arithmetic as 'showing great inaccuracy', the reading as 'monotonous' and the results in higher subjects as 'extremely meagre') half the children passed in arithmetic, over half in writing and about two-thirds in reading. Between 1880 and 1884, nearly all the children passed in reading and the averages for writing and arithmetic were about two-thirds.

There were always problem families whose children could be relied upon to fail consistently, which brought the examination averages down so George White had to take such pleasure as he could in the few children who stayed at school longer than their contemporaries and showed a greater aptitude: children like Mary Briggs, for instance, who stayed in school until she was 16 in 1879, and Pearson Rigg and Tom Edmondson who in 1881, aged 13 and 14 respectively, 'answered fairly in Botany and pretty well in Physical Geography'. And he had to search for such rare words of praise bestowed by Claude Parez as (in 1884): 'The order is good and the manners of the children are pleasant'. But he could not have looked forward to the annual ordeal of inspection and report.

Loweswater school group 1931

SUPPLY AND DEMAND[1]

In April 1879, the Rev. George Mercer Tandy, in his vicarage at Loweswater, received the kind of bureaucratic communication that all Trustees and Managers of Schools sighed over. Circular No 176, a three page (foolscap) letter from the Education Department in London, was a copy of Guidance to H. M. Inspectors of Schools on the requirements for the needlework examination.

Needlework was a subject taught in schools like Loweswater's to all girls. In some schools it was taught to boys as well - a practice the Education Department was keen to encourage. During the year, various garments were made and had to be produced to the Inspector (an early kind of continuous assessment) and there was also an examination at the end of the year. This examination took between 45 and 60 minutes during which pupils undertook various exercises. At Stage 1 - the simplest stage - pupils fixed various types of hem; by the most advanced stage - Stage 6 - pupils were darning, patching, embroidering letters and cutting out frocks for babies.

What would probably have made Mr Tandy groan was the footnote which stated that school managers had to ensure a 'full supply of candles, cottons, scissors, thimbles etc. and paper (newspaper or ruled to show selvedge) for cutting out. Each child should also have a label showing her name, age and the stage for which she is presented, which she must affix to her work when finished'. The supply of these materials -for the examination and throughout the year - was clearly a source of keen anxiety for Mr Tandy.

First he tried T. W. Gatey of Keswick (linen and woollen draper) who in July 1879 supplied him with 34 yards of grey calico at 4½d a yard, 24 yards of white calico at 7½d a yard and 4 reels of white cotton at 2½d each. Evidently, either the quality or the price was not satisfactory; the following year he went as far afield as Newton, North Wales, where he patronised Barrington, Morgan and Co's Royal Victoria Warehouse. (Manufacturers and Merchants, Real Welsh Flannels, Shawls, Homespuns, Tweeds, etc.) However, grey calico was ½d a yard dearer there and a couple of years later he was buying at Robinson Brothers in Cockermouth. ('Wholesale and retail Woollen and Linen Drapers, silk Mercers, Haberdashers etc. Funerals furnished.') The next year, he was off to Wilfred Graham, 28 Main Street, Cockermouth where he got his white calico more cheaply but had to pay 14d a yard for the hideously expensive white flannel. A year later still, he found a better bargain at Wm. Elliot of Cockermouth ('Linen and Woollen Draper').

Other supplies for the school proved less difficult to obtain. Mr Tandy found regular reliable suppliers in D. Fidler of Main Street,

---

[1] First published June/July 1990

Cockermouth ('a parcel from London every Thursday') and Nelson and Sons of Paternoster Row, London. From Fidlers, he bought stone jars of ink (2½ pints) every half year, three boxes of pencils a year, two boxes of pens, exercise books, foolscap paper, envelopes. Textbooks came chiefly from Nelsons but some from Fidlers too. Loweswater pupils learnt from *The Royal Reader, The Brief History of England* and Steadman's *Grammar Helps;* they read *The Last Chronicles of Barset* and Scott's *Lady of the Lake.*

When it came to cleaning, whitewashing the schoolroom and general maintenance, Mr Tandy patronised businesses nearer to home. Originally, coal for heating was provided by W. C. Iron and Steel Co. Ltd. (Cockermouth Coal Depot) who supplied either Melgramfitz or Lowther coal. Mr Tandy took the former at 6½d a cwt. Unfortunately, the cartage charge was five shillings. Coal was a very big item in winter; in January 1879, for instance, Mr Tandy ordered 17 cwts, in March a further 15 cwts and in April 16 cwts more. Every penny he could save therefore counted and he found a better deal with T. Dickinson who was based at Ullock Station - 6d a cwt for best coal, and three shillings and sixpence for cartage.

As far as structural repairs were concerned, Mr Tandy had no need to go out of the parish, dealing with blacksmith Joseph Beck (aged 32) at Gillerthwaite and William Norman, the 54 year old joiner at Jenkin Hill. In 1879, Beck supplied two holdfasts and nails (one shilling), a pump handle, spear rod and various screws, bolts and nails as well as a new fireguard (weighing 17 ½ lbs). William Norman was generally called upon to replace glass, eleven panes in all between December 1878 and November 1880 which suggests that children were much the same then as now.

All this - and the salaries of the master and mistress (about £90 for the master alone) - had of course to be paid for. The school had been endowed by its founder, John Marshall, MP and Lord of the Manor, with £100, which yielded a regular income. There was also an allotment of common which the school rented out and for which they received at first £6 10/- every half-year. Unfortunately, the rent for this tended to go down rather than up; by 1881, it was down to only £4 5s per half-year.

The Education Department provided a grant for the school based on the number of pupils who attended and who took the examinations. This was dependent on the yearly inspection being satisfactory. In addition, the parents of each pupil paid a quarterly fee known as School Pence and this raised about £9 10s a quarter. The trouble with both these sources of income was that, depending on pupil numbers, they varied from year to year and were therefore unpredictable.

The fact that education, though intended to be universal, was not intended to be free, is emphasized by a receipt signed by George Tandy in 1882. 'Rec'd July 6th, 1882, of the Master and Mistress of Loweswater School, £1 2s 6d for articles of clothing made by children at the school and sold to parents of the same'. The parents too ultimately paid for Steadman's *Grammar Helps* and *The Brief History of England.*

Of course there must have been parents who refused to buy the books and clothing, and who were tactically deaf when it came to requests to pay School Pence. Mr Tandy could not by law force them to pay. According to a memorandum from the School Attendance Committee for the Cockermouth Union sent to the Managers and Teachers of schools in their district in 1884, parents who refused to pay their 3d a week could not be taken to court for recovery of the fees. All that could be done was to refuse the child admission and then proceed against the parents for their child's non-attendance. Meanwhile, Mr Tandy had to try and balance the books. Being the Trustee or Manager of a school was not an enviable job.

The school after the 1950s conversion to village hall

The Kirkstile Inn, Loweswater – photo by permission of the Kirkstile Inn

The Scalehill Hotel, Brackenthwaite, around 1900

PASTIME WITH GOOD COMPANY[1]

Sometimes you just know you're going to enjoy yourself. Take New Year's Day, 1843, for instance, when the inhabitants of Loweswater and Buttermere had the annual hunt and ball of Mr Nelson to look forward to. The reporter from the Carlisle Journal was there and 'the day being fine, a large number of sportsmen assembled' with the hounds of Mr Head of Matterdale – 'and a prime pack they are'.

Unfortunately, the foxes were coy on this occasion but as the huntsmen caught three hares, that was some consolation and there was much pleasure still to come. 'The hardy sons of Nimrod then repaired to the house of Mr Nelson where a sumptuous dinner was awaiting their arrival and was partaken of by 150 persons.' After dinner came dancing in the ballroom 'where a large number of the fair sex were assembled, when dancing commenced which was kept up with great mirth and good humour' (and possible some indigestion) 'until an early house in the morning.' The revellers, the *Journal*'s journalist said, were 'highly pleased' with the entertainment.

There have been organised entertainments since man first sat round the cave fire at the end of a day's hunting for food. In medieval days, such entertainments would have been centred around religious feasts; in later days, more secular entertainments have developed – hunts and hunt balls, whist drives, dances, the show of course, and a miscellaneous selection of 'other events'. There are dangers associated with fun however; as everyone knows, frivolous doings are dangerous to the soul and occasionally to the body as well.

Quakers knew this only too well, although younger Friends sometimes had difficulties in prising themselves away from the temptations of the world. Pardshaw Monthly Meeting records contain an apology from John Harrison in March 1712.

> *Since it hath happened that there has been rude Works in my house of latt which have been a great trouble to me and to friends in general about fidling and dancing and such vanity which truth canat alow of I am very sorry that it hath happened so to the grefe of faithful Friends which I am willing to condem and promas with truth that ther shall be noe more such worke if I can help it.*

Earlier, in 1705, Quakers had warned 'such young Friends as frequent Markets and fairs to wear such modest or decent Apparrell as becomes their holy profession'. There was a more serious side to this advice however. Quakers were often resented and feared by other sections of the

[1] First published April/May 1991.

community and, in the same Minute, Friends were warned that 'both men and women, be careful not to go in great companies together in Markets and fairs, to Inns and places of resort or Otherwise ... and to forebear walking together in such great Companies for the future', for fear of provoking adverse reactions from other fair-goers.

In 1821, too much indulgence in a good time was literally the death of John Wilson of Mockerkin. 59 year old John went to market in Cockermouth on 25 August but did not return home. After an anxious search, his body was found in a river near Southwaite, early on Tuesday morning. Exactly what had happened will never be known but his friends, knowing the habits of his horse and the fact that 'he had drunk rather freely' supposed that on his way back home he had fallen asleep and 'tumbled off his horse when the animal stopped to drink in going through the water'. A freak death, but Quakers would have insisted that John Wilson brought it upon himself.

Some organised entertainments were opportunistic, with an edge of hard necessity to them. In February 1895, unemployed men in Loweswater seized the opportunity offered by a very heavy frost and snow, to erect an 'ice house' (igloo?) on the frozen-over River Cocker. By charging for admission, they earned a considerable amount. The following year, September 1896, the inhabitants of Loweswater judged it profitable in a slightly different way, to mark a wedding in extravagant style.

> *Marshall, Muckley: At White Notley Church, Essex, on the 5th Inst by the Rev. A Curtis, assisted by the Rev. S.A. Marshall, brother of the bridegroom, William Hibbert, eldest son of Walter J Marshall, of Patterdale Hall. To Lenore Fairfax, younger daughter of Mr Muckley of White Notley Hall, Essex.*

The father of the groom was Lord of the Manor in Loweswater. In a last fling of feudal loyalty, the inhabitants of Loweswater lit a huge bonfire on 'the lofty head' of Burnbank and 'sent its bright rays far across the surrounding countryside'. The bride – 'an artist of much merit' according to the Carlisle Patriot – was well known and popular in Loweswater 'with all classes'. Her health and the bridegroom's were drunk 'amid much cheering and firing of guns all round'.

Lest it be thought that the adults had all the fun, the Carlisle Patriot quotes two occasions in 1896, when the Loweswater children were entertained in thorough style and were expected to enjoy themselves – though the second occasion was probably more popular than the first.

In April 1895, the inaugural meeting of the Loweswater Band of Hope was held in the schoolroom. In charge were the curate, the Rev. J. M. Collinson, the teachers Mr George White and Miss Bell, and the curate's wife, Mrs Collinson. There was a good turnout of about 40 children 'who had been enrolled with the consent of their parents'. As this seems to represent virtually all the valley's children, it is probably that many were rather too young to appreciate what was going on.

A prayer, a hymn and then the Rev. Mr Collinson reached the real business of the evening, preaching a rousing address on the evils of intemperance and urging the children to be total abstainers for life. Finally he informed them that they would be able to enjoy such meetings on a monthly basis from then on, including further instruction on temperance and the learning of recitation and songs. Sadly, it is not possible to trace how long the Loweswater Band of Hope remained in existence or how effective it was.

Six months later, the children were meeting again for an extra-curricular activity that was almost certainly more to their taste – the Loweswater children's treat – their annual field day. Mr Collinson was to the fore again, as was the head teacher, Mr White, together with Mr Storar Jackson and Mr Tindal Jepp.

When the children arrived at school at 2 pm on a rather overcast, heavy-skied afternoon – it was to see a see-saw, an 'Aunt Sally' stall, posts and nets set up for various games and a stall organised by the Girl's Friendly Society who were willing to sell to friends the work they had made over the last few months. The girls flocked to the see-saw, the boys to games of football and cricket. There was a programme of races of various kinds, which had to be fitted in between heavy showers but most were successfully run before a huge shower of hailstones interrupted proceedings. Fortunately, this coincided with tea time.

After 'a substantial tea ... partaken of by the children', the remaining races were run on the road, because of the soggy condition of the field. No doubt there were some undesirable effects of this exercise being taken after a heavy meal.

And then, of course, there were the prizes, for which the winners had to wait only a little time, while Mrs Collinson explained that the money raised from the sale of good by the Girls' Friendly Society (£3 11s 6d) would go to Mrs Chalker of Carlisle towards her fund for maintaining a home for friendless girls. And with that reminder that there should always be a serious reason for having fun, the party dispersed.

ON THE FIDDLE[1]

Everyone knows that the best tunes belong to the devil - or so the Quakers thought.

> *'Since it hath happened that ther hath been Rude Works in my house of latt [late] which have been a great trouble to me and to friends in general, about fiddling and dancing or such vanity ...'*

In 1711/12 John Harrison of Pardshaw Meeting wrote a note in eccentric spelling (even for the times) apologizing for ungodly goings-on in his home. Almost a century later, Peter Robinson of Lorton came to a very similar state of mind. Peter was a carpenter and, according to Mrs Anne Lancaster who had known him when he was a child, 'in his younger days, [he] had been a fiddler and was reckoned a good one'. With maturity came rather more seriousness. Peter became a 'religious man' and, according to rumour, burnt the fiddle. Rumour, fortunately may have been false in this case as in the 1880s it was said that Peter's fiddle survived in Mayo Street, Cockermouth along with his 'big fiddle' which may have been the fiddle's larger brother, the viola.

There was a well accepted tradition, at least in Lorton and Loweswater, that religion and fiddle-playing did not mix. Music in church services consisted of singing religious texts - not hymns but metrical psalms - unaccompanied. At Lorton, the choir in 1819 consisted of two families - the Ewarts and the Pearsons plus the parish clerk and Mrs Woodhouse of the Green, described as 'a terrible fine lady'.[2] Most frequently, the clerk and Mrs Woodhouse found themselves singing a duet. (Mrs Woodhouse was described by Mrs Lancaster not as the 'best' but as the 'leading' singer at the church which may not necessarily have been the same thing.)

As a child, Anne Lancaster was a fascinated witness of the singing of these psalms and to the 'prelude' to them:

> *Old Tom Crosthwaite [the clerk] was great on these occasions. Dressed in his best black coat - narrow sleeves, with bright buttons and short-knee breeches, a large shirt neck coller with a black neckerchief on - Tom would stand up to give out the psalm ... then he read the first two lines ... then he straightened his coller, blew his nose, blew the pitch pipe and raised the tune.*

---

[1] First published March 1993.

[2] The Green was approximately where Lorton Hall Lodge now is, but closer to the river. Mrs Woodhouse was once Isabella Fletcher, who had married a gentleman. Ed.

The pitch pipe bore no resemblance to the pitch pipes obtainable nowadays for tuning instruments. It was literally a single pipe of a recognised pitch which was blown to give the singers a note. (It is interesting to speculate whether this led to every psalm being started on the same note.) Both the pitch pipe at Lorton and that at Loweswater - a square pipe - had been lost by the 1880s.

At Loweswater church there was rather more ceremony to the singing of the psalms. The clerk would first march down the aisle and climb up into a gallery at the west end. From there he could announce the psalm and the congregation would turn their backs on the priest so that they could sing facing the choir in the gallery. 'Loweswater singers', says Anne Lancaster, 'were considered good ones.' Certainly Thomas Cowper, chaplain at Loweswater a little before Anne's time, was moved in 1757 to write a special poem in the church register on the death of Ann Bank of Low Park whom he described as 'a charming singer of psalms'. He wrote: 'Sweet Harmonist, who died in youthful days/ Thy life was one continued hymn of praise.' Again, it would be interesting to know if Thomas was simply using the word 'harmonist' in its general sense as 'musician' or in a more specific sense as 'one skilled in harmony'. In other words, were the psalms sung in unison, or did some people, including perhaps Ann, sing harmonising parts?

Much as fiddling and religion didn't mix, there were plenty of opportunities to indulge outside church. Anne Lancaster (Anne Iredell in those days) used, as a child, to attend dancing lessons with her brother. The classes were held in a room upstairs at the Rising Sun Inn in Lorton.

> *Our dancing master was Mr Carrodus. He was a fiddler as well and he went up and down the country teaching. He was a smallish man and wore pantaloons, not knee breeches and they came down to his ankles and were tied with tapes, so they didn't fash him when he was dancing. He had pumps and white stockings.*

Pantaloons were the latest fashion (being the forerunners of trousers) so Mr Carrodus was apparently very up-to-date. However, 'he got vexed sometimes,' Anne said, 'and gave the boys slaps'.

If the children and no doubt adults too, who attended these lessons, wanted to show off their new found skills, they might have a chance at one of the clipping days when, after all the sheep were shorn, food was accompanied by great merrymaking. Songs were certainly obligatory on these occasions and singers used to go from one clipping day to the next with their favourite ditties. The popularity of the singers was not always according to the quality of their voices. One of the great favourites was

John Fletcher of Lorton who had a thin quavery voice.[1] He would invariably sing: 'Tarry wool is ill to spin but may be clothing for a Queen'.

Dancing however was chiefly on display at the Merry Neets. These were evenings promoted by innkeepers, ostensibly for the simple pleasure of young people although, as was pointed out, the innkeepers made a great deal of profit from them too. At Lorton, the most famous Merry Neet was at the Pack Horse on the evening of Candlemas Day. Dancing was the main reason for attending; men had to pay two shillings, and women and lads one shilling. Often, people who did not go sent their entrance money for fear of being thought miserly. The fiddler at the Merry Neet was the only musician – 'there was no such things as a piano or harmonium in the whole fell-side,' said Anne Lancaster. He was paid by a subscription taken during the evening.

The Merry Neet at Scale Hill was generally around Christmas or New Year and their fiddler was Richard Bowman from Lamplugh described as 'a capital fiddler'. Richard was also the leader of the 'carol singers' at Loweswater on Christmas Eve.

These singers started on their rounds just before midnight so that Richard always began by playing a raucous lively tune called the Handsrup to wake everyone up. Then the singers would sing a carol especially personalised by the addition of the names of the people being visited. One verse for every occupant could make the carol a long one, but was nevertheless much appreciated. The family would then be entertained by a hornpipe or other similar tune – both played and danced – and then another verse or so and off the carol singers would go. They would get their reward at the Merry Neet at Scale Hill when the families they'd serenaded would bring along money and pies for them. Wordsworth of course wrote a poem about the custom:

The Minstrels played their Christmas tune,
Tonight beneath my cottage eaves …
Keen was the air but could not freeze
Nor check the music of the strings.

---

[1] John (Auld Doc.) Fletcher, the veterinary, had the farmstead which in the 1840s would become the Wheatsheaf. Ed.

Chapter 4: LOWESWATER FAMILIES

This selection of articles illustrates the pusuits and experiences of family historians, covering the sources of information and the practice, with the problems, in the context of Loweswater and its families, other than Quaker families. What is striking is how family history practice has changed in the short time since these articles were written. The sources are the same but the internet in particular has made the sources accessible and in particular allows the censuses from 1841 to 1901 to be searched from home in seconds. Gone are the shoe-boxes and the card indexes - except for the 'traditionalists'.

Roz does not have Cumberland ancestors and therefore has no particular family of interest. Instead we have here, and in other articles, a good coverage of traditional Loweswater families, as seen though the surviving family records, plus a helpful discussion of the sources from parish registers and records, censuses, wills, manorial records and other property records. But also a family historian needs to know a good bit about the practices in the locality, which are well covered.

Family history is easiest where families do not move much, and 'sequestered' Loweswater was a customary manor with a good number of yeoman families. The customs guaranteed that the farmstead, or tenement, could be inherited, and in Loweswater tenements were mostly handed down in families, but sometimes through a daughter. Quaker holdings were even more likely to be kept within family or friends.[1] But increasingly in the eighteenth and nineteenth centuries, yeomen sold their farms and they were let to the more mobile farmers. Mining families came and went with the mines.

Illegitimacy is often found locally and makes life difficult for family historians. From around 1750 it became more common in Cumberland rising to around 18% of baptisms at its peak a hundred years later. Marriage required an income and a house to support the large families that resulted. Cumberland developed quite sophisticated poor-law and family support arrangements which seemed to reject the lack of humanity in Malthus' insistence that a woman who was poor should also be derived of the opportunity of being a mother. Many had one child, never married, and lived and worked within the community. The children fared as well as legitimate village children.

---

[1] Loweswater is studied in **Winchester, Angus J L** Wordsworth's pure commonwealth, Yeoman dynasties in the English Lake District c. 1450-1750 *Armitt Library Journal* 1/1998 pp 86-113. Ed.

QUESTIONS AND ANSWERS[1]

Investigating family trees can be a fascinating pastime but it does have its down side. You go off to the record office/churchyard/library with a clean untouched notebook and a newly sharpened pencil and come back with hundreds of apparently unconnected names and a headache from eye-strain caused by trying to read the hurried scrawl of a sixteenth or seventeenth century curate. Another few hours sorting and you realise you now have far more questions than you started with. And most of them are for ever unanswerable.

Take, for instance, the Parish Registers which reveal that between 1817 and 1819 no fewer than six illegitimate children were born at Pottergill, on the lower slopes of Low Fell. With the exception of twin girls, all the children were born to different and unrelated mothers. Was this, you wonder, the local house of ill repute? Or was the house so isolated that girls 'in trouble' were sent there by their parents until their children were born.[2]

The registers start in 1626 and provide a full account of births, marriages and deaths, including the place of residence of the families concerned which is very useful. Until, that is, 1632, when the registers suddenly stop. They don't start again until the 1670s; family trees just begun hang in mid-air during Cromwell's time when the official line was that the keeping of registers was not a matter for the church. In 1673 Mr Patricius Curwen, the new curate, did his best to rectify matters. 'The register is imperfect,' he writes apologetically and goes on 'The rest of the Christenings, marriages and burials done until the 17th Oct. An Dom 1665 looke the old Register Books where you will find them written.' Unfortunately, he adds: 'The old register is lost.'

And it's no good going to the churchyard to try and fill the gaps. The earliest gravestone (half illegible) dates from 1695 and even after that they can be puzzling in the extreme. On the gravestone for the Mirehouses of Miresyke John Mirehouse is recorded as dying in 1807 at the age of 101 years. In 1706, however, his presumed date of birth, his mother Mary – according to the same gravestone – would have been seven years old. There's something wrong there somewhere ...

There are local papers, of course, which supply the researcher with interesting snippets of information, such as the size of hailstones in 1775 and the number of mutton pies eaten in Buttermere at Christmas 1774 (850). On

---

[1] First published August/September 1987.

[2] Pottergill was the last property in Loweswater in the hands of the trustees of the late Joshua Lucock Bragg of Lorton Hall. A marginal farm, it seems to be used at this time by the poor law guardians of Loweswater for maternity and lying-in for poor single mothers. After purchasing Pottergill in 1824, John Marshall combined it with his Rigg Bank land. Ed.

family matters, these papers supply useful detail: the *Carlisle Patriot* records, for instance: 'a few days ago was married at Loweswater Mr John Hudson of Kirkgate to Miss Fanny Fisher of Coldkell, a fine young lady with a genteel fortune.' What was a 'genteel' fortune? This is one question which does have an answer: Fanny's sister, Anne (known as Nancy) was married two years later and was described by the *Patriot* as 'an accomplished young lady with a fortune of £1000' - a substantial amount for the eighteenth century.

Back to the registers for a few more answers for fans of the man who used to write to the Times about the most popular children's names of the year. Between 1626 and 1632, the registers show that only a limited number of names were used in Loweswater registers. Boys were most likely to be called John (used 25 times) or Thomas (10 times) or William (8). For girls, Jennet (16) and Annas (7) were most popular. After that irritating gap, the registers start again in 1773 and over the next two decades there is a definite change. John is still the most popular name for boys and Mary, just, is most popular for girls, but there is a much wider range of names in use. There is a biblical flavour too, with Isaac, Aaron, Moses and Benjamin, Rebecca, Martha and Mary (twins), Debora and Susanna.

Fads surface from time to time. In 1626, girls might be called Ellin; in 1629 this disappears totally in favour of Ellinor. In 1684, six boys were born - two were called Thomas and the other four were called John. In 1686, all three girls born were called Mary.

The average number of births per year in the late 1620s was 13 or 14 with two years reaching 20 births. Oddly enough, the increase in these years was in boys; in most years the number of boys and girls born was fairly even, with fractionally more boys being born than girls - usually about 7 to 8 or 8 to 5. In the 1670s and 1680s, however, the birth rate fell to an average of 9-11 per year, with an occasional high of 15.

But of course all this raises more questions. How large was the population in the valley? How many of these children died when young? Were girls more likely to survive than boys or vice versa? Did the decline in the birthrate continue and if so, why?

Ah well, back to the records.

LOVE AND MARRIAGE[1]

Entries in parish registers tell only the most basic of facts about an event. When Jenet Iredell married in 1681, did she marry for love? Did she grieve when her husband Nicholas died in February 1685/6? Did she look for consolation to William Mirehouse when she married for a second time in October 1687?

The answer to all these questions is almost certainly no. Jenet was probably only 14 years old at her first marriage and her husband was over 40. When he died, she was still only 19, with two very young children and a farm - Pottergill - to manage in trust for her 18 month old son. She needed a second husband badly. When she was widowed for a second time, she was nearly 40 and her son an adult who could farm for himself. She did not marry again.

Jenet Hudson of Kirkgate on the other hand may well have married, at least once, for love when her first husband, Thomas Bragg, died in March 1681/2. Their daughter Annas was only a year old but Jenet had a close family - she was her father's heir and still lived at home. She didn't need to marry, making it more likely that her second marriage, eight years later, was a love match.

Evidence showing whether people in Loweswater married for love, convenience or comfort in past centuries, is difficult to find. Take the case of Thomas Mirehouse of Sosgill for instance. In July 1705, his maid, Jane, gave birth to their child, a daughter; their marriage only took place five months later. Did they marry for love? Or under pressure from relatives, neighbours and parish authorities? When, three years later, little daughter Jane died, Thomas was quick to name his next child after his wife, who argues a strong degree of affection.

Ironically, six years later, the younger Jonathan Dixon, a Quaker, also caused uproar for the sake of love when he went off with his housekeeper. For her sake, he was baptised into the Church of England and married her on the same day. He was of course at once disowned by Quakers and brought his two children up as Anglicans. His elder child, Sarah, returned to the Quaker faith however and her marriage was certainly one of convenience. At the age of 30, in 1805-6, she was 'wooed' by a fellow Friend, Joseph Rooke. A letter he wrote to his sister, Mary Iredell of Thackthwaite, shows a distinctly pragmatic approach to the match:

'The person I shall allude to,' he wrote, 'appears to be the most suitable, but I am quite at a loss to get an introduction.' Had Joseph not even spoken to his intended bride before he chose her? He clearly did not know her family background very well as he continued: 'If thou already knows her to be engaged, the object must fall to the ground, the which I

---

[1] First published November 1992.

should feel sorry for.' Joseph was not to be disappointed however - in 1806, he bore his bride off to Newcastle.

Of course, lust and love have been constantly confused throughout the centuries. In the late 1820s and early 1830s, parish registers show approximately one illegitimate birth a year; later in the century, illegitimate births were usually followed very quickly by a marriage. Sometimes the marriage came, just, first. In many cases, the relationship may have been a 'trial' marriage, that is, a couple intending to marry merely delaying the actual ceremony because of financial or family problems.

In other cases, marriage was plainly never in mind. Matthew Dickinson of Thackthwaite clearly never intended to marry Ellinor (or Ellen) Wilkinson of Thrushbank before or after she gave birth to their son Francis in May 1826. The birth may even have been concealed from Ellen's family and neighbours for a while as the child was baptised at Crosthwaite. Eight months later, when Ellen was dying, she left all her few possessions to her son and did her best to ensure that Matthew had no say in her son's upbringing. Any love between the pair had obviously long since disappeared. Two years later, Matthew fathered another illegitimate son, Peter - the Loweswater registers do not record the mother's name.

By far the most complicated love-life seems to have been enjoyed(?) by Anthony Robinson. Early in 1620/1, Katherine Mason of Crosthwaite parish gave birth to his daughter, Jenet, but marriage - to Katherine at any rate - was not in Anthony's plans. He had another lady in mind - Isabel Thwait of Newlands, whom he married in 1622. Isabel died less than a year later, however, and Anthony proceeded to enjoy his newly-refound bacherlorhood. In 1627, he fathered a son, John, and in 1630/1 a daughter, again called Jenet. (The names of the mothers are again not recorded.) Not until 1632 did Anthony remarry, to Margaret Wilkinson of Loweswater at which point, the parish registers abruptly stop, making it impossible to tell if Anthony settled down and confined his activities to producing legitimate children. It seems unlikely.

For the great love-match, it is necessary to return to the Dixons, to the father of the Jonathan mentioned above. John Dixon was 30 years old when he fell in love with Anne Woodville, the daughter of his neighbour; she was 19. Quite apart from the complication that he was a Quaker and she was Anglican, there was one, apparently insuperable, bar to their marriage. They were too closely related. John's aunt, Jenet, was Anne's grandmother - that brought them within the prohibited degrees.

Quakers and Anglicans alike forbade the marriage. John and Anne took matters unto their own hands; on 21 April 1690, they went off to Cockermouth, found a credulous priest (or one who asked no questions), and were married.

How the Church of England reacted is not recorded. Quakers at Pardshaw Meeting were outspoken. They condemned John for 'want of watchfulness and not keeping the Fear of God in ye lowliness and humility of his mind.' He had not 'kept nor walked as becomes the truth nor in unity with his people'. In language that makes Anne sound like a scarlet woman, they said: 'he hath suffered his mind and affections to goe out after a woman of the world .... she being one of his near relatives which is not justifiable before God nor the sons and daughters of men which woman he hath now married and that with a priest'. They agreed to disown him.

The sequel is interesting. With a promptness and a sincerity that seems suspicious considering he had now had his own way, John apologised to the Quaker Meeting for his error and they agreed to accept him back into the Society. Nothing more was said about the validity or otherwise of the marriage; John and Anne lived together for thirty years and had five children, all of whom were brought up as Quakers. John's widowed mother lived with them until her death in 1705. There seems to have been no suggestion that the marriage should be set aside as illegal. Which suggests that Anne and John had probably judged the situation correctly when they decided to act first and apologise later.

FAMILY MATTERS[1]

The Pearsons at Loweswater were many and various, occupying houses such as High Cross, Latterhead, Stockbridge, Watergate, Bargate, Iredale Place and Fangs. They appear in manor court records, parish registers and wills in such profusion and with such similar names that it is difficult to separate one family from another and decide who was related to whom.

They make their earliest appearances in records belonging to the Earls of Northumberland who owned Loweswater for some time in the Middle Ages. The Pearsons here provide a fascinating insight into the origin of surnames. In 1429, Peter Johnson was granted the fishery of Crummock Water; in 1480, the same fishery was granted to William Pereson Johnson and it becomes obvious that he is Peter Johnson's son or Pe[te]reson. Does this mean, I wonder, that Peter's father was called John? It certainly means that there could be a number of Peresons in the parish with no relationship to each other or anything in common except their fathers' Christian name.

At about the same time, the Pearsons are appearing in manor court records. In 1457, John Peyrson Dicson appears on the jury (was his father Peter and his grandfather Richard?) A couple of years later, Thomas Peyrson was complaining that John Jackson owed him money.

Later still, there was a John Peyrson at Millhill and a Henry Peyrson at Watergate. At Whynfell in 1519 lived another John Peyrson, a miller who seems to have been unscrupulous as he was accused of demanding too much payment for milling his customers' corn - but then millers were always being accused of such things.

Late in the 16th century, the first surviving wills from Loweswater appear; the earliest known Pearson will dates from 1623. John Pearson lived at Fangs - the will mentions a wife, Ellin, and two sons, William and John. The elder John was probably of a reasonable age when he died as both his sons had children of their own, but the Pearsons of Fangs were a family whose menfolk tended to die young. The William Pearson who died in 1711, for instance, was probably only in his 40s; his youngest child had been born merely two years before. After a long minority this son, John, came into official possession of the estate (yearly rent £1 6s) and shortly afterwards in 1733 married a Mirehouse of Myresyke. Parish registers record the birth of a daughter, Hannah, in February 1736, but there must have been a son too, another John. At some time in the summer of 1736, with his daughter only a few months old, John died. He was 27 years old and the family entered on another long minority.

Another will was made at Fangs in September 1648 by Jennet Pearson, the widow of John - it is possible that she was the widow of the

---

[1] Originally published in two parts in January and February 1995.

son John mentioned in the will of 1623. But their names appear nowhere else that I can trace and only their daughter Margaret makes an appearance in the parish registers. The problem here is that the family lived at the time of the Civil War when church registers were very patchily kept; in Loweswater there is a gap from 1633 until about 1673. So the births and major life events of Jennet's children, John, Matthew, Thomas, Peter, Christopher and Robert, as well as Margaret, are, at the moment, impossible to trace.

Jennet was certainly wealthy. She left £20 to each of her children (except the eldest son who would inherit the estate) and also bequeathed them various pieces of furniture, a table, a grate and (fire) basket and a bed to her eldest son, an 'arke, a table and all other things' in the family's property at Buttermere to another son.[1] Margaret inherited all her mother's clothes 'both linen and woollen'. The inventory of Jennet at her death shows clearly that she had been actively involved in farming.

The Pearsons of Fangs were clearly thriving but there was another family down in the valley whose history shows the problems associated with having large families: principally, what was to be done with younger sons?

Thomas Pearson of Watergate had at least four children between 1627 and 1632 – that gap in the parish registers after 1633 means that he may well have had more. One of these children, John, married Ann Iredell from Braiththwaite and had nine children. The oldest two were born at Bargate, the next five at Iredell, and the last at Watergate, the children all being born over a period of only 11 years. The repeated moves made by the family suggests landless labourers moving where the work was.

Incidentally, some ambiguity of surnames survives even at this very late date; when one of John's daughters was buried in 1696/7, the parish registers referred to her as 'Ann Iredell'. Was she an eldest daughter, perhaps born before her parents' marriage, or had she simply chosen to take her mother's name? And, if the latter, why?

Another Pearson, possibly a son of John's, was Robert, baptised in 1686. He makes an appearance at Iredale in 1714, then by 1716 was back nearer the family home, at Stockbridge. Three children later, he moved to Latterhead. At Stockbridge he was described as a shoemaker, at Latterhead as a farmer.

Unfortunately, parish registers show that the previous tenant at Latterhead had been a Robert Pearson, and that in 1695 he had a son also called Robert. The course of events becomes hopelessly confused. (Was the Robert who moved to Latterhead in 1719 the son of John of Watergate after all?) He was certainly the same as the Robert of Stockbridge – children who

---

[1] *Arke* – a meal-ark; a container with a domed lid for holding the family's supply of oatmeal. Ed.

were born at Stockbridge are recorded as dying at Latterhead. But who was the Robert who had been at Iredale in 1714? Had that been the Robert of Latterhead or of Watergate? If Robert of Latterhead was the son of the previous Robert there, what happened to the Robert who had been born at Watergate? And if he was the Robert of Watergate what happened to the Robert born at Latterhead?

Sorting out who was who in the family becomes even more difficult when you take into account the Pearsons of Thackthwaite, Iredale and Kirkstile (another wandering family with six children born between 1684 and 1702), and the prolific Pearsons of Mockerkin. The family of John of Mockerkin consisted of nine children between 1669 and 1688;[1] John and his wife went through a biblical phase when naming their middle children, calling them Joseph, Aaron, Mary and Joseph again (the elder Joseph died aged 4). Another Pearson family of Mockerkin, that of Thomas, had six children four of whom had the same names as four of John Pearson's which leaves ample room for more confusion.

The most 'aristocratic' Pearson of the time - and the most mysterious - is John Pearson of High Cross, the only member of the clan to be accorded the 'Mr' in the parish registers. As such, he was probably a landowner with independent means who did not need to work for a living. But all that is known of him otherwise is that he married a Deborah Wood from Lamplugh and had at least three children, one of whom did not survive infancy. He died in 1735 at the age of 53 after only nine years of marriage.

One Pearson, Isabella of Mockerkin, must surely hold the record for the longest will made in Loweswater, with 41 separate bequests benefiting 45 named people and an unknown, but certainly large, number of others represented by such bequests as 'to the poore of Loweswater', and 'to the rest of Thomas Pearson's children' and 'to every servant in Mockerkin'. There can hardly have been a family in the parish who did not benefit.

Isabella, who made her will in 1645, was a widow who apparently had no children. Her brother, Nicholas Mirehouse of Sosgill, still lived, as did his son Gilbert (who seems to have been a rogue and received not even the proverbial shilling in the will). Isabella also seems to have had two sisters, both married but now dead - she left legacies in her will to her brothers-in-law and nephews and nieces. What Isabella had in abundance, however, were godchildren.

Ten godchildren are mentioned by name - eight Isabellas, one Peter and one John - but so many other unrelated children feature in the will that many must have been godchildren too. Each godchild was left a sum ranging from 2s 8d to ten shillings, and their brothers and sisters were all

---

[1] Although there may have been more children - that gap in the registers causes problems again.

each left a smaller sum. Then after 36 provisions, mostly of this kind, provision 37 says: 'And to all the rest of my godsons and goddaughters not named 2s. 8d a piece.' Half the children of the parish must have had Isabella as a godparent.

What made Isabella so popular in this role? Was it a cynical wish to feature in the will of a childless widow? Some of the godchildren however were plainly adults with children of their own (often Isabella's godchildren too) and Isabella must have stood sponsor for them long before it could have been certain that she would be a rich widow. Moreover, Isabella was plainly not a soft touch. In the will, John Jackson was told very plainly that his four children would only get their one shilling each if he paid back to Isabella's executors the sum of forty shillings that he owed her. It is not recorded whether John paid, or whether he reckoned that he would be better off keeping the forty shillings and giving his children a shilling each from his own pocket.

And finally, Isabella disposed of her household goods which seem to have been few. A grate in her house was given to a man who was probably her nephew; one of her brothers-in-law received 'the frame standing in the ... house'. A loom? A bed? Isabella had previously conferred with a friend, Margaret Wilson, about the disposal of her clothes and in the will simply asked Margaret to 'deliver all my cloathes which is shapen to my backe unto any persons as I have nominated unto her'.

There was nothing else.

THE MISSING LINK[1]

One of the pleasures of investigating local/family history is finding other people with similar interests. So I was interested to come across a plea for help in the magazine of the Cumbria Family History Society. Someone was investigating the Cass family at Loweswater.

The couple in question, from Ipswich, were related to Ada Cass who used to live in High Lorton. They had traced their family back to the beginning of the 18th century and there the trail seemed to go cold. So I dug into my shoeboxes of index cards and into my envelopes of census returns and my general files. And this is the story so far …

One of the golden rules to be followed in trying to trace your family tree is to work backwards from what you do know to what you don't. For instance, if you know that your grand mother married in 1900 at the age of 20, you can consult the records for 1880 to find her birth. That will give you her parents' names. Then you can look for *their* marriage which with any luck will tell you their ages and then you can in turn look back for their births. Deaths should not be neglected however; many a promising family tree has fallen down after the discovery that some supposed great-grandfather had in fact died aged 3.

The best place to look for the Cass family in the late 1880s is the census. The 1881 census shows them living at Thackthwaite. Joseph Cass was an agricultural labourer and eight years older than his wife Mary who had been born in Blindbothel. Three sons were living with them at the time: Joseph (aged 13), John (10) and Fearon (7). All three boys were at school - officially. A glance at the school records, however, shows otherwise. Only John appears there, in 1878 and 1879, when he was 8 and 9 years old. John's attendance was only moderate - he was present about half the times the school was open. In 1878 he passed his writing and arithmetic but failed reading; in 1879, he failed writing but passed the other two. He entered the school in August 1877 but there is no sign of him only three years later and his brothers never appear in the records at all.

Also living in the house at Thackthwaite were four other people - a kind of extended family. One was Mary's daughter - though it is not clear whether Mary had been married before or whether this daughter was illegitimate. Certainly, the daughter, Joyce Ritson (aged 26) was herself an unmarried mother with two small children - Mary (aged 4) and Henry (aged 2). The fourth person was James Ritson who may have been a brother or brother-in-law of grandmother Mary.

Working backwards, the 1871 census reveals that Joseph and Mary had had four older children who by 1881 had grown up and left home. After three daughters - Sarah (or possibly Dinah - the census is difficult to

[1] First published January 1994.

read), Eleanor and Frances - came another son William. There were fifteen years between the oldest and youngest children and the youngest, Fearon, was only three years older than his niece, Joyce Ritson's child.

And further and further back ...

Joseph, according to the parish registers was baptised on 21 October 1826. He was the son of William and Sarah Cass at Pottergill and was the oldest member of the family, with four younger sisters and a brother. His mother seems to have died quite young; his father, William was a widower by 1851 and had moved to Thackthwaite - he may have moved as early as 1829.

William himself was born in 1800, the son of Henry and Eleanor Cass who had moved three years previously. He seems to have had a sister, Frances, who in 1825 gave birth to an illegitimate son, Henry. The father was named in the parish registers as John Iredell of Red Howe.

And there the trail abruptly stops although not, hopefully, for ever. The obvious records - parish registers, manor records etc have no information for the Cass family for the period between 1747 and 1797. However, further back still, there is a little island of fact, that - perhaps - is relevant.

In 1711, the parish registers record the marriage of Thomas Cass of Bargate to Sarah Wilson. A year later, their eldest son, Sollomon [sic] was born. Two years later, Sarah gave birth to a daughter but sadly the child lived less than six months. Perhaps Sarah gained some consolation from another daughter born in 1717 and a son born in 1720 but in 1724 tragedy struck. Sarah gave birth to twins in March - they were so sickly that they were baptised at once (by the midwife?) in a private baptism at home. The twins were buried only four days after their birth.

The family lived at Bargate but Thomas was not a farmer but an agricultural labourer. Towards the end of his life, he must have grown infirm - the parish registers recording his burial in 1748 describes him as a 'poor' labourer which certainly means he was receiving relief from the parish because of his inability to work.

Thomas and Sarah's only surviving daughter, Deborah, married three years after her father's death. She was 27 years old - about the average age of marriage for a woman in Loweswater at the time. Her bridegroom was Edward Simpson at Stockbridge who was a shoemaker. Almost exactly a year after the marriage, Deborah gave birth to a daughter, named for her mother, Sarah, and two years after that had a son, Joseph. But something must have gone disastrously wrong with that second birth; Joseph was baptised on 4 September and buried only two days later. Deborah was buried eight days after that, aged 30.

Was this Cass family the ancestor of the later family? The heads of both families were agricultural labourers, landless and probably frequently teetering on the edge of poverty. Perhaps the Christian names of the respective families will help - family trees in Loweswater families show again and again the use of a limited number of names for family members with the occasional infusion of new female names because daughters were often named after their mothers and maternal grandmothers. Unfortunately, the evidence here is inconclusive. The later Casses show this pattern; William (used 3 times), Joseph (twice), Eleanor (twice), Frances (three times), and Dinah (twice) are the only names used. In the earlier family these names do not occur. Thomas and Sarah were a devout couple and named their children for Biblical personages. They had a taste for the Old Testament, using Isaac and Jacob (for the twins), Deborah, Jonathan, and Solomon (surely a hard name to live up to?) The only exception was the daughter who lived only six months and was named Grace.

Lacking any other evidence from which to draw conclusions, the only thing to do is to reserve judgement and to keep looking for those missing links that might, one day, complete this particular family saga.

PEOPLE AND PLACES[1]

When you are planning your next holiday, forget all about Skegness or Brighton. Catch the ferry to Boulogne, instead, and climb the hill to the old town. Outside the high town walls, in the middle of grass and flowerbeds you'll come across a statue of an elegant gentleman, his eighteenth century clothes freshly painting, standing on a tall stone plinth.

On one side of the plinth, there's a French inscription which reads: 'This statue was erected by the town of Boulogne sur Mer and the Society of Industrial sciences, Arts and Belles-Lettres of Paris in honour of Edward Jenner, discoverer of Vaccination. It was inaugurated on 11th Sept 1865.'

But it's bit of a cheat really; Jenner (even if he was the discoverer of vaccinations - some say Lady Mary Wortley Montagu brought it to England half a century before him) should not be on this plinth. Which is possibly why his expression is faintly uncomfortable. Because on the main face of the plinth, right under his nose, is the name of the real hero of the hour - Dr William Woodville, originally of Loweswater.

'William Woodville,' the inscription says, 'Physician at the Smallpox Hospital of London brought to the French people, despite a state of war, the discovery of Jenner and made the first inoculations at Boulogne sur Mer on 27th Prarial, An. VIII.' [The Revolutionary way of writing 19th June 1800.] 'The vaccine gathered by Dr Nowel was sent to Paris where Woodville carried out inoculations on the 1st of Thermidor following.'

This is the only monument (to my knowledge) erected in honour of a native of Loweswater. Don't miss it!

---

[1] First published December 1990/January 1991.

Chapter 5: PROPERTY AND HOUSES

The articles in this chapter are about places in Loweswater, both natural features such as hills and watercourses, and the settlements and agricultural lands that were created and needed to be identified. The historical study of place-names in the lakes can give insights into the relationship between the patterns of settlement and the ethnic origins of the settlers, as *What's in a name?* shows us. Recently, Diana Whaley has published the academic study *A dictionary of Lake District place-names*, which has allowed a couple of names to be updated in notes. In Cumbria, the successive waves of settlement have added to rather than replaced the earlier settlements and so the incomers often, but not always, respected the existing names. The British names for rivers and some hills remain; the Anglians (no Saxons here) spread from Northumbria, giving us Lorton, Embleton and Brigham. Then the ethnic Norwegians, already settled in Western Scotland and Ireland, came in a negotiated settlement, mainly from Ireland, in the early tenth Century. Loweswater is full of Old Norse names.

Of cooking pots and monks is in this chapter because it addresses the organic element of boundaries, how they were 'drawn' to reflect existing patterns of settlement and land use and how they change over time. Every wiggle in a boundary is there for a reason which can either lead to fascinating information from the past, such as why Graythwaite is an outpost of Mosser, or a puzzle such as how the Loweswater boundary moved from Warnscale Beck to Sourmilk Gill. Boundaries delimited the ownership of resources, and for the early church the setting of parish boundaries also set their income from tithes. The inclusion of Loweswater and its chapel in the parish of St Bees c.1125 gave the monks the tithes, but also included were land, rights and property, including the predecessors or sites of the mill and the Kirkstile - until the dissolution.

Disappearing tricks charts organic decline through the buildings that were lost in or around the nineteenth century. By 1800 Loweswater had lost both its fulling mill, in favour of Lorton, for the reducing cloth manufacture, and also its corn mill. After 1850 a shift from arable to stock required fewer people, fewer and larger farms, and as a consequence buildings became redundant. Mining was not sustained and Loweswater had neither the good communications nor the proximity to Cockermouth which allowed Lorton to diversify and retain its infrastructure. Loweswater lost people, buildings and arable land, which is probably why, when the new civil parishes and ecclesiastical parishes came to be formed, Loweswater crossed the Cocker and gobbled up a large part of poor Brackenthwaite; a meal shared with Lorton and Buttermere. Roz introduces us to the people who lived and worked in some of the lost Loweswater properties.

WHAT'S IN A NAME?[1]

Students of prehistory can climb chilly mountain sides to excavate collapsing heaps of stone; historians of the Middle Ages and later can hurry off to the warmth of Carlisle Castle to peer at disintegrating parchment and old newspapers. But what can you do if you're interested in that so aptly named period from the departure of the Romans until the Middle Ages begin - the Dark Ages. No stones, few documents - what's left?

Place names.

When the Romans pulled out of the area in the third and fourth centuries AD, they left the native Celts living in hillforts and remote valleys. A couple of centuries later, along came the Anglo Saxons. They were not too keen on valleys filled with forest and swamp and cold winds; they liked the fertile pastures around places like Buttermere - the word is Old English for 'the lake by the dairy pastures'. They christened the Cocker too (the crooked river)[2] and Crummock Water (the lake of the crooked water), Foulsyke (the muddy stream or ditch) and High and Low Hollins (the place where holly bushes grow).[3]

No doubt they had names for other local places but these have not survived. In the tenth century along came the Norsemen in large numbers than the Anglo-Saxons could deal with. No rape and pillaging here, as on the East Coast of England, these Norsemen were farmers. They were used to hard conditions and could take advantage of any farming land even if they had to chop down forests to get at it.

Their usual procedure was to establish farms on fertile lowland. Lorton (probably 'the farm by the roaring stream') could have been one of these. From this farm in summer the flocks would be sent out to what were known as shielings - summer pastures higher up the valley. In the winter sheep would come back to the farm. Scale Hill comes from the Old Norse for 'the shieling on the hill''. Whiteside means 'the white mountain shielling'.[4]

As years passed, permanent farms would be built up at these shielings and the flocks would be sent still further up the valley, to Mosser, for instance ('the shieling on the peat moss'). And so gradually the valley

---

[1] First published October/November 1987.

[2] The names of hills and rivers are sometimes British, and predate both the Anglian settlement of C7th & 8th and the ethnic Scandinavians of the early C10th. The Cocker, Koker around 1170, is thought to be 'the crooked one' from the British 'kukra'. Whaley 2006 p.76. Ed.

[3] All definitions are taken from Lake District Place Names by Robert Gambles.

[4] Specifically, Scales comes from Old Norse *skali*, huts, which would be found on the summer pasture. *Saetr* is ON for sheiling or summer pasture, and sometimes becomes seat (Lord's Seat) and sometimes side (Swinside). *Erg* is the Gaelic-Norse sheiling or summer pasture as in Mosser. Ed.

would be colonised, though the population would probably have been smaller than it is nowadays.

Most of the place names in Loweswater and the surrounding area come from the Old Norse. Many are purely descriptive, like Rannerdale, 'the valley of the ravens' and Lanthwaite 'the lone clearing'. There are some surprises; Pottergill for instance is unlikely to be named after someone who made cups and saucers –'pot' or 'potte' is Old Norse for a deep hole of pool. Loweswater itself is 'the leafy lake'.

Other names hint at the kind of life the settlers of the valley lived. Thackthwaite was the clearing where reeds grew for thatching; Latterhead probably means 'the headland with a shelter for farm animals'. Gillerthwaite was 'the clearing where snares are set'[1], and Carling Knott was 'the hill where the old woman lives'.[2]

Cinderdale Common, even so early on, was known for its industry; Coledale means 'the valley of the charcoal burners'. Gatesgarth, beyond Buttermere, has nothing to do with gates, and everything to do with enclosures for goats – thus explaining too the Goat Crag overlooking Buttermere. A little further afield, Ullock was definitely the place *not* to go – the name means 'the place where wolves play'.

Of course we shall never know for certain just what life was like in Loweswater at such an early date. There are very few clues in this detective story – but it's fascinating to guess!

---

[1] The *gill* in Gillerthwaite in Loweswater and elsewhere is uncertain and may come from ON *gildra* for 'snare', or ON *gilra* 'of streams'. Being so close to the open arable fields and also to a possible more neucleated original centre, the snares seem unlikely, but also gills are usually streams in a ravine. Ed.

[2] If this is the case, the 'old woman' may be one of the oldest characterised inhabitants of the area.

OF COOKING POTS AND MONKS ...[1]

I made my New Year's resolution when I found, in two books on local history, the term 'subinfeudated manors'. I resolved immediately never to use jargon, or at least not without explaining what I mean.

Resolutions are of course made to be broken, but I've made a few more historically speaking, or rather I've made a list of topics I'm resolved to investigate this year in the hope of clearing up a few mysteries.

Firstly, there is the matter of the erratic course of the parish boundary as shown on OS maps. At first sight it looks straightforward: along the River Cocker, down the edge of Crummock Water, over the fells to Mockerkin, along the fells back to Thackthwaite and the Cocker forming a roughly triangular shape enclosing all the different sorts of terrain - lake, arable, woodland, common - that inhabitants might need. A closer look however reveals some perplexing details. For instance, the boundary makes the most peculiar of wiggles to include one of the Holme Islands at the Buttermere end of Crummock. Why? It dips into Waterend to remove Graythwaite from the parish. Why?

Nor does it follow the Cocker along the entire course; behind Redhow Woods it briefly meanders away from the river into what might logically be expected to be Brackenthwaite - several more times it repeats this trick on the way to Lorton. Such antics are usually a sign that the river has changed course, either accidentally or through human agency. But when? (And while we're in this area of the map, the boundary between Brackenthwaite and Lorton around Birkett Cottage looks as if it was drawn by a mad doodler.[2])

The parish boundary was probably settled in the misty early days of the Middle Ages, as was, perhaps, the site of the church. Documents survive in the archives of St Bees Priory dating from the 12th century describing the parish and the monks' title to it. Richard Lucy evidently gave the Priory monks pasture in his forest (Loweswater was probably part of the Forest of Copeland at the time) for twenty cows, one bull, and their offspring. The monks could also take trees necessary for building and burning (that is, for fuel). Fish, poultry and pigs were also dealt with in the deed - but it is in Latin and my knowledge of Latin is distinctly rusty; I resolve to improve it.

Other documents in St Bees' possession deal with Sorescal (or Sorestal or Soureschallis) and Mokerkyn (or Mokerkins or Molkorklyn)

---

[1] First published February/March 1990.

[2] The manor of Brackenthwaite was subinfeudated out of Derwentfells in the C12th and the boundary was established as the cultivated lands of Lorton. See Winchester - *Discovering parish boundaries*. Brackenthwaite had the boggy parts uncultivated by Lorton. Ed.

better now known as Sosgill and Mockerkin, and with 'Thakthwayt'. Loweswater was 'Louswatyr'.

Coming a little more up to date, I'd love to know more about Millhill. For a start, what kind of mill was it? There appears to be no stream near it on the ground or on the map to make a water mill, although of course the original mill may not have been on the same site as the present building. This would appear to indicate that it was a windmill but that would be unusual indeed for this area.[1]

A house certainly existed at Millhill in 1457 when its tenant John Jackson was fined for poaching. In about 1488, Robert Hodgson was fined for 'going away from the mill' that is, going to another mill to have his corn ground. Tenants were supposed to have their corn ground at the local mill but if the miller was avaricious (as many were reputed to be) and took more than his fair share of corn as payment (multure), many farmers went off to another mill in the hope of a better bargain. Just to prove the point, Robert Pearson, miller in Whinfell, was fined in 1520 for taking more multure than he was entitled to.

To add to the confusion, papers belonging to the Earls of Northumberland show that there was a fulling mill in Loweswater in 1439 (rent 28/-) and in 1483 (rent 21/-). Fulling - a method of finishing cloth to make it waterproof and more durable - had been carried out in water-powered mills in Cumbria as early as 1135 AD.

In the latter half of the 17th century, there seem to have been about three families at Millhill at any one time, all with good Loweswater names - Walker, Burnyeat, Willkinson, Iredell. By 1753, Joseph Skelton of Foulyske owned the site and was fined for allowing the road 'leading from the said Lords Mill' to fall into disrepair.

There are more intimate matters which I'd also like to investigate, like clothes and cooking pots (Jenkyn Dicson brought Thomas Pele to the manor court in 1459 for 'the breaking of one cooking pot') and furniture. Details of what people wore and the goods they used domestically are few. The inventory of William Dixon of Waterend (taken in 1734 after his death) mentioned his 'purse, apprill [apparel] and rideing gear' and his books. Otherwise, unfortunately, it simply refers to 'goods in the Parlor'. 'goods in the fire house' and 'goods in the Bakehouse loft' and so on.

A little later, in 1810, James Muncaster of Thackthwaite left to his wife Mary his 'household Goods and furniture of implements of Household, Beds, Bedsteads, beddings and Hangings Linen and Woolin'. When Mary died the following year, she left her son Jonathan £100 and her silver spoons. Her sister, Sarah Wood, received Mary's best black quilted

---

[1] The myth of the Loweswater windmill has no substance other than the name, Millhill. While the miller's house was at Millhill, the mill itself, the lord's mill, would have been near the foot of Mosedale Beck. A survey is needed. Ed.

petticoat, her best little hat and cloak. Her daughter-in-law, wife to another son, Henry of Netherclose, received Mary's best woollen cloak. The rest of her 'wearing apparel of Linnan' was to be divided equally between her surviving grand-daughters. Unfortunately, after all this detail on her clothes, she simply refers to 'my household furniture'.

Mary also mentions her debts, 'whether on Bond, Note or otherwise'. Being in debt at this time was not unusual, not discreditable but quite in the normal course of events. William Dixon's inventory, for instance, reveals that William owed a total of £121 - a substantial sum; however, he was owed by friends and neighbours a total of £382 so his books more than balanced. This system of debts owed and owing seems to have been a way of spreading risk amongst your own ventures and other people's. William also had two shares in ships, apparently sailing from Whitehaven, and these were worth £30. He was not the only parishioner with an interest in shipping; the extent of the interest is another thing I'd like to find out.

Oh, and finally, I resolve to find out exactly what is meant by 'subinfeudated manors'.[1]

Bargate, early twentieth century, before it was destroyed by fire. Bargate was a fulling mill, out of use as such c. 1800. The earthworks in nearby Tenters field were probably associated with the tenter riggs

[1] Subinfeudation means that a feudal lord gave or sold part of a large manor to another person, who became lord of the smaller subinfeudated manor. For example, Brackenthwaite was subinfeudated out of Derwentfells manor (the forest between Cocker and Derwent) in the twelth century, and later came under the same lordship and administration as the manor of Loweswater. Ed.

DISAPPEARING TRICKS[1]

Things are always disappearing. The most recent examples are the milk stands which once stood at the top of the lane to every farm, but it surely cannot be long before the bus shelter at Jenkin Gap keels over backwards into the bushes. Not the prettiest of objects but nevertheless an historical artefact.

Disappearing tricks are not a modern phenomenon. The prehistoric village at the foot of Grasmoor for instance is only visible from above in the driest of dry weathers and only the slightest of signs remain of the (British? Norse?) settlement between Scale Force and Crummock Water, where once there were huts and enclosures and fields cleared of stones for planting. In medieval times, so some documents say, there was a chapel of St Mary Magdalene at Rannerdale, but information about the chapel is so elusive that it is tempting to think it a figment of someone's romantic imagination.

In the Middle Ages too, a manor house - probably a pele tower - stood on the edge of Crummock, on the promontory that bears the name of Peel today.[2] The remains of a moat can still be traced but any buildings have long since vanished. The original was probably wooden; a stone successor was plundered to provide material for cottages that stood there until the late 19th century. These were home for weavers - 'websters' as the parish registers call them - and tailors. One came to a tragic end as John Jackson the parish clerk recorded:

> *John Pearson of Peel. He was supposed to be blown off the road at his coming from Buttermere by an east wind on the 3rd day of May 1818 and was buried on the 20th May 1818. Aged 48 years. He lade 27 days in the water and was found above Rannerdale Lodge by John Tyson of Gillerthwaite and Joseph Grindal of Lanthwaite.*

The last recorded inhabitant of Peel was Ann Briggs, a forty year old widow who lived there in 1871. According to the census of that year, she had three children, Thomas, aged 13, Abigail 11, and Mary 8. All the children had been born in Dearham and Ann herself was from Abbeyholme so she was a relative newcomer to the parish. The 1881 census records Peel as being uninhabited.

Once upon a time, of course, all villages had a mill. In Loweswater, the name Millhill (originally Milnhill) commemorates a mill owned in the

---

[1] First published June/July 1989.

[2] Thomas de Lucy, lord of the manors of Loweswater and Brackenthwaite, created his seat here c.1300 and extended the park which had been taken in from the common by his father, Alan Multon, who had married the heiress Alice de Lucy. See Wilson, 1915. Ed.

1750s by Mr Joseph Skelton of Foulsyke. The age and exact position of that mill are difficult to trace, but another mill, at Brackenthwaite, certainly existed in the 16th century.

This mill stood at the edge of the road near Low House and saw its share of excitement. In the 1650s, it was the subject of a heated dispute between the Lord of the Manor, Sir Wilfred Lawson, his tenant, William Clemettson, and an interloper from Loweswater, Robert Fisher.

Apparently, in 1652, the mill was derelict and Robert Fisher took it upon himself, without licence from the Lord (at the time Sir Wilfred's father) to repair it. The Lord objected. An arbitrator was appointed to look into the matter and both Robert and the Lord agreed to adhere to the arbitrator's decision; if either party failed to do so, they were to pay a fine of £30. In addition, Robert was warned to keep away from the mill site until the arbitrator had reported, on pain of a further £30 fine. Robert promised faithfully to obey - and promptly went back to Brackenthwaite and started to 'worke upon the aforesaid Mill and Millstead in that the said Robery caused slate to wit, 20 loads of Slate to be placed and dressed upon the Millstead aforesaid'.

It is surprising that the Lord of the Manor continued to object to the improvement of the mill, particularly since Fisher was obviously at the time and expense of the repairs. For some reason, Sir Wilfred took seven years to get round to doing something about this outrage, this 'plotting and fraudulently intending to deceive and defraud'. In 1659, he brought Robert to court, complaining that Robert owed him £40 for damage done to the property. At the same time, William Clemettson also brought an action against Robert. Clemettson claimed that Sir Wilfred had granted him a seven-year lease of the 'water-corne mill called Little Mill and one acre of land with appurtances' with effect from 2 February 1657. According to Clemettson, Fisher 'did eject, expel, and remove' him, causing £10 worth of damage.

Robert pleaded not guilty and was given time to reply, that is, to offer a defence. Unfortunately, no more documents referring to the case survive; local history is full of fascinating half-stories.

The mill escaped the disastrous floods of 1760 when the stream on which it stood, the Liza, burst its banks; the force of the water was by chance deflected to the opposite bank. On an OS map of 1863, the mill is shown, still as a water corn mill - and there the trail stops.

There are a number of farms which are now no more than names and perhaps a barn marking the spot. A line of three - Bargate (reputedly burst down in or around the First World War), Millhill and Stealbank - lie along the bottom of Melbreak; two more - Riggbank and Pottergill - are situated just off the Thackthwaite road. Riggbank is marked by a now ruined barn at the road's edge between Foulsyke and Cold Keld; Pottergill is a heap of stones at the foot of Low Fell.

Riggbank certainly existed in the early 17th century, when the occupants were John and Isabel Fisher. The registers record the birth to them of at least two children, Margaret (born 1627/8, died 1630) and Peter (born 1632). Peter survived but plainly was not on the best of terms with his mother; in 1662, she complained that he had thrown her out of the half of the house to which she was entitled as a widow.

After that, there are only names scattered in the parish registers to suggest who lived there: Elizabeth Piel (died 1714), John Hodgson, farming there in 1719. In 1784, John Fisher of Cold Keld complained that John Grainger was trespassing on Riggbank land by 'Making way over different parts of the said tenement from Foul sike to Potter's Gill'. John Fisher would hardly have been complaining unless he had some interest in the land; as far as I can tell, however, he was no relation to the John Fisher who farmed there in the 1620s.[1]

It is impossible to say exactly when Riggbank was last inhabited. An estate map of property belonging to Sir Wilfred Lawson (a descendant of the 1659 baronet) in 1807, shows that there were no buildings whatsoever on the Riggbank land; any dwelling house had been demolished. Sir Wilfred's successor as Lord of the manor, John Marshall, drew up his estate map in 1819; again, no house is shown and one of the few references to the property in John Marshall's correspondence simply says: 'The field Rigbank was drained by Henry Muncaster [for many years John Marshall's bailiff] but it was unsuccessful' (1843).[2]

Pottergill lasted longer. In the registers the first reference to it is in 1666, when it was tenanted by a family of Mirehouses, first Jennet (nee Iredell of Latterhead) and her husband, Nicholas, then Jennet and her second husband, William Mirehouse. Jennet and Nicholas's son, Thomas, continued in possession until well into the next century.

The Marshall estate map of 1819 records the owner of Pottergill at that time as Raisebeck Lucock Bragg, Esq. (a splendid name - I'm sorry I don't know more about the owner of it).[3] Pottergill must have been a traditional long house with a house at one end and barn at the other. The

---

[1] John Fisher was bailiff for the Lord of the Manor; he may therefore have been objecting on the Lord's behalf.

[2] A lord of the manor is missing here, but he lasted only two years. The manor of Loweswater, including the lake and Holme was sold to Joshua Lucock Bragg of Lorton Hall in 1807, born Joshua Lucock and grandson and heir of the Joshua Lucock who built Wordsworth House. He died in 1809, the estate handled by his three trustees. They sold the manor to John Marshall in 1814, with Rigg Bank but not Pottergill, which Marshall acquired in 1824. Ed.

[3] Raisbeck was the eldest son of Joshua Lucock Bragg, who left six children with wife (and cousin) Rebecca in Lorton Hall. Four, including Raisebeck, were or became lunatics. The trustees were kept busy by Chancery cases until the last Lucock Bragg, in care of attendants, died at the hall in 1875, leaving only ghost stories. Ed.

original approach was by a track from Latterhead, but a mid-nineteenth century map made by John Marshall when he acquired the property, shows a path from the road near Riggbank, perhaps along the route John Fisher had complained of. Living conditions must have been primitive, at least until 1837, when Joseph Lancaster, the local builder, undertook alterations on John Marshall's behalf.

Joseph's account of expenses details the work that was done. The old chimney was taken down (1½ days work at 3/3d per day) and all the old materials carted off (4 days work costing 13/-). A new 'chimney-peace' was inserted (5 days work costing 16/3d) and a new grate put in (16/3d) plus a boiler (16/3d). An oven and another grate were installed (16/3d), the roof was repaired with new timbers (a total of 9/9d) and various walls replastered and rendered (9/9d). The total bill came to £11 15s 7½d and the work was done between the 8th and 22nd December, so the winter was presumably mild that year.

The beneficiaries of all this work were the Banks family. Joseph Banks had married Mary Muncaster, daughter of Henry, John Marshall's bailiff - perhaps that was how Joseph obtained those much needed repairs. Mary died in the 1850s but Joseph and his children - Henry (aged 27 in 1861), Mary (21), Joseph (19), Jonathan (14) and grad-daughter, Mary Ann (aged 2) - continued to live at Pottergill until well into the 1860s. By 1871, however, they had moved to Netherclose and Pottergill was occupied by Isaac and Sarah Jackson, their son John (1½ years old) with three agricultural labourers as lodgers. In 1881, a family called Cartmell lived there, but there had obviously just moved in; their children, including the youngest, Sarah, aged 7 months, had all been born outside the parish.

And there the story of Pottergill ends, until the 1891 census is released - or someone reading this article can give me more information.[1]

And finally ... Spout House, the ruins of which can still be seen at the junction of the roads to Askill and Miresyke. Spout House was occupied by Wilkinsons for at least three centuries until sometime between 1851 and 1861. The house was then taken over first by the Hunters (John Hunter was an agricultural labourer) and then by Harrison Walker, who described himself as a gardener. John Wilkinson, the census enumerator, lived at neighbouring Miresyke until the 1870s; his successor as enumerator, William Iredell of Red Howe, records in 1881 that the only family of Wilkinsons in the parish resided at Place. Spout House was uninhabited.

---

[1] Pottergill was uninhabited in the 1891 census, with a note 'temporarily absent', but by 1901 it was not listed. Ed.

Chapter 6: LORDSHIP AND AUTHORITY

In the previous chapters Loweswater has been portrayed as a self-contained and self-regulated township, but Loweswater was not an independent republic. This chapter covers the external relationships of supervision and authority, and the resources of Loweswater that were due to be paid or used.

A pre-industrial English village such as Loweswater had three long-established systems of supervision and control, each with its own court and officers; the manorial system, the church and the state. The manorial system controlled property and land use. The manor of Loweswater was the property, granted by the crown, of the lord of the manor. The manor had a boundary and the customary tenants had rights to use their farmsteads or tenements subject to the customs of the manor, plus rights on the commons . The relationships among tenants and between tenant and lord, who each had rights and responsibilities, were managed through the Loweswater manor court and its officials, covered by the first three articles.

The church building, or at least the nave, was the property and responsibility of the church wardens but the clergy, a curate in Loweswater chapel, were appointed from outside. Mockerkin and Sosgill were in the chapelry boundary, but not in the manor, having been lost to Derwentfells in the late middle ages. The clergy, supported by the church courts, had authority in moral and religious matters, though by the eighteenth century the Church of England did not have the control of either the Pardshaw Quakers or the other 'dissenters'. Writing notes in the registers most have been some consolation as *In clerkes finded written*.

The third external line of control was the state, which gradually took over as the other two diminished in importance. The long transfer to the state of church authority and responsibility dates, of course, to the reformation, but in Loweswater the manorial system functioned well into the twentieth century. John Marshall and then William resisted enclosure and division of the commons for nearly forty years, and on eventual enclosure in the 1860s Marshall did not enfranchise the tenants, keeping the property customary. The statutory systems involving assizes, magistrates and constables are not covered in articles, but the local institutions, rates and taxes focussed on the township, and its successor the civil parish. This forms the subject matter of *Taxing times*.

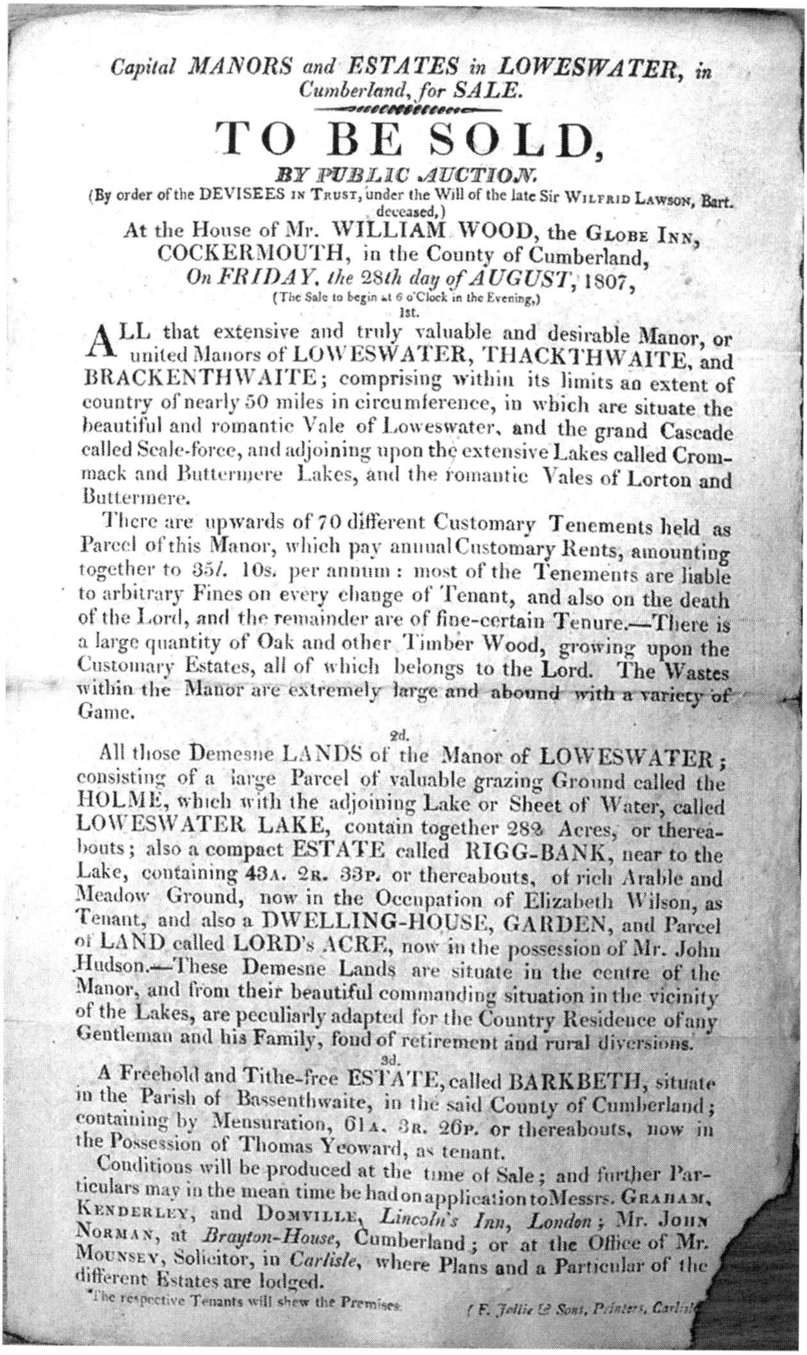

Capital MANORS and ESTATES in LOWESWATER, in Cumberland, for SALE.

TO BE SOLD,

BY PUBLIC AUCTION.

(By order of the DEVISEES IN TRUST, under the Will of the late Sir WILFRID LAWSON, Bart. deceased,)

At the House of Mr. WILLIAM WOOD, the GLOBE INN, COCKERMOUTH, in the County of Cumberland, *On FRIDAY, the 28th day of AUGUST*, 1807,

(The Sale to begin at 6 o'Clock in the Evening,)

1st.

ALL that extensive and truly valuable and desirable Manor, or united Manors of LOWESWATER, THACKTHWAITE, and BRACKENTHWAITE; comprising within its limits an extent of country of nearly 50 miles in circumference, in which are situate the beautiful and romantic Vale of Loweswater, and the grand Cascade called Scale-force, and adjoining upon the extensive Lakes called Crommack and Buttermere Lakes, and the romantic Vales of Lorton and Buttermere.

There are upwards of 70 different Customary Tenements held as Parcel of this Manor, which pay annual Customary Rents, amounting together to 35*l.* 10s. per annum: most of the Tenements are liable to arbitrary Fines on every change of Tenant, and also on the death of the Lord, and the remainder are of fine-certain Tenure.—There is a large quantity of Oak and other Timber Wood, growing upon the Customary Estates, all of which belongs to the Lord. The Wastes within the Manor are extremely large and abound with a variety of Game.

2d.

All those Demesne LANDS of the Manor of LOWESWATER; consisting of a large Parcel of valuable grazing Ground called the HOLME, which with the adjoining Lake or Sheet of Water, called LOWESWATER LAKE, contain together 282 Acres, or thereabouts; also a compact ESTATE called RIGG-BANK, near to the Lake, containing 43A. 2R. 33P. or thereabouts, of rich Arable and Meadow Ground, now in the Occupation of Elizabeth Wilson, as Tenant, and also a DWELLING-HOUSE, GARDEN, and Parcel of LAND called LORD's ACRE, now in the possession of Mr. John Hudson.—These Demesne Lands are situate in the centre of the Manor, and from their beautiful commanding situation in the vicinity of the Lakes, are peculiarly adapted for the Country Residence of any Gentleman and his Family, fond of retirement and rural diversions.

3d.

A Freehold and Tithe-free ESTATE, called BARKBETH, situate in the Parish of Bassenthwaite, in the said County of Cumberland; containing by Mensuration, 61A. 3R. 26P. or thereabouts, now in the Possession of Thomas Yeoward, as tenant.

Conditions will be produced at the time of Sale; and further Particulars may in the mean time be had on application to Messrs. GRAHAM, KENDERLEY, and DOMVILLE, *Lincoln's Inn, London*; Mr. JOHN NORMAN, at *Brayton-House*, Cumberland; or at the Office of Mr. MOUNSEY, Solicitor, in *Carlisle*, where Plans and a Particular of the different Estates are lodged.

The respective Tenants will shew the Premises.

(F. Jollie & Sons, Printers, Carlisl

Advertisement for the sale of Lowswater manor and lands, 1807. by permission of Waugh & Musgrave, Solicitors

ANCIENT AND LAUDABLE CUSTOMS[1]

Anthony Patrickson of Stockhow, Ennerdale, Lord of the Manors of Loweswater, Thackthwaite, and Brackenthwaite until his death in 1627, was neither a patient nor a prudent man. Money seems to have slipped effortlessly through his hands so it was hardly surprising that he decided to put up the rents on his properties. The rents had been static for many years and were now ridiculously low. He also thought that selling one or two of the woods he owned might be a good idea and, while he was at it, he would prevent his tenants from taking valuable trees - as they had from time immemorial - for 'house-boote, fire-boote, plough-boote, gravel garve and hedge-boote, and cart-boote, etc'.

It does not appear to have occurred to Anthony Patrickson that his tenants might not much like his ideas for making money. They were prepared in fact to take him all the way to the Court of Chancery in London where in 1597, even more to Anthony's surprise, three eminent judges found against him, agreeing with the tenants that he 'did ... go about by diverse indirect means contrary to all right, equity and good conscience to alter, innovate and change at his own will and pleasure the complainants' ancient and laudable customs'.

The result of this judgement was that over the next few years Anthony came to agreements with his tenants in the various manors, which set out exactly what these 'ancient and laudable customs' were. At least one of these documents - an agreement made in 1598 with the tenants of Brackenthwaite - survives in the Cumbria Record Office and together with Manor Court Rolls, provides a fascinating glimpse into landlord-tenant relations at the time.

Eight tenants made the agreement with Anthony Patrickson: Robert Syubb, John Rudd of Pickethow, Thomas Rudd, John Tolson, a joiner at Low House, John Rudd of Beckhouse, another John Tolson, Lawrence Mireshouse and Robert Rudd. (The repetition of names is confusing and shows the limited number of families in the area.) These men and the men in Anthony Patrickson's other manors, held their land by a 'perpetual Certaine reasonable and Ancient Custom' called 'Tennantright'. In return for being ready to ride out and face any Scots who dared to maraud into Cumberland, the tenants were free men, not subject to the usual feudal requirements, renting all their land for their own use, not being obliged to work on the Lord's demesne as men elsewhere in England were forced to do. (There is a theory that this custom grew up because early Lords of the Manor thought that tenants would prefer to run for their lives rather than fight for their Lord's estate; if they rented the land for their own benefit, however, they would be more likely to stay and defend it.)

---

[1] First published February-March 1989.

Rents for the properties, unhappily for Anthony Patrickson, remained low after the 1587 court case. Walter Iredell, for instance paid 17s 11d for his tenement at Waterend; Peter Burnyeat paid 4s 2½ d for Pottergill. These rents were paid three times yearly (at the Purification, Pentecost and St Martin) and in addition every tenant had to pay 'due custom and service' to the Lord by turning up at the yearly Court held for that purpose (usually at Gillerthwaite for the three manors, occasionally at Churchstyle i.e. Kirkstyle). Yet at the same time, the Brackenthwaite agreement clearly states that the tenants had the right to 'alienate, give or devise' the property, that is, to sell the land, or bequeath it to their descendants - a provision normally associated only with ownership of a property.

Admittedly, there were conditions attached to this concession. Properties for instance had to be bequeathed to the oldest surviving son or daughter or their heirs - it could not be divided up between several sons. But the great advantage of the system as far as the Lord of the Manor was concerned, was that he continued to obtain income from the property while ensuring that tenants kept the land in good heart, motivated by confidence that they were building up a property that could be enjoyed by their children.

The records of that yearly court at Gillerthwaite, the Manor Court, survive in an almost unbroken series from 1713 till 1794 and show the system still working efficiently two centuries after Anthony Patrickson's time.

At the court, a jury of local people 'presented' to the Lord's steward all the local business with regard to land. This included bequests, sales of land and any quarrels over ownership or boundaries, or such things as water supplies. Two affeasors set the level of fines for anyone found guilty of an offence. Constables to keep law and order were appointed by the court, as were Viewers of the Common who were supposed to make sure no one overgrazed the common or used it for illegal purposes. All these people, with the exception of the Lord's Steward, were local people and fines therefore tended to be low; it didn't pay to be hard on offenders. One year you might be an affeasor, the next you might be accused of an offence and the last thing you'd want was to see in court someone you'd fined heavily the year before.

The first entry in the Court Rolls - an isolated entry for 1662 - demonstrates another aspect of the agreements Patrickson made. The entry reads: 'Isabell ffisher widd[ow] did present Peter ffisher (her son) for disturbing her of her possession of her widdow right in a certain place called Riggebanke lately in ye possession of John ffisher her husband deceased contrary to ye custome of Loweswater'. Turning back to the Brackenthwaite agreement of 1598, we find a provision that a widow 'of full age' was to have half of every tenement her husband had 'owned' so long as she did not remarry. For this property she was to pay 'a God's penny to the

Lord for the same' - what we would nowadays call a peppercorn rent. The court accordingly found that 'ye said Widd. ffisher shall have halfe of ye tenement which John ffisher her husband enjoyed'.

Other matters of inheritance were more straightforward. As per Patrickson's agreement, sons or nearest male relatives usually inherited. Thus in 1717, the jury found 'Thomas Iredale of Thackthwaite his death and John Iredale his son heir'. In 1756 John Dickinson inherited from his grandfather, in 1723 Thomas Wilkinson was bequeathed Spout House by his brother Jonathan. From time to time an entry shows how hard and how short life could be. In 1724 for instance, an entry reads: 'We find an infant unbaptised heir to his father Philip Burnyeat of Thackthwaite'. In such cases, Patrickson's agreements stipulated that the property should be administered by two of the minor's next-of-kin, that it should be leased out (sub-let, in effect) and the profits applied to the minor's education. If next-of-kin were for some reason unavailable, there was provision for four neighbours to carry out the same tasks.

Perhaps contrary to expectation, women do not come off too badly legally under this system. Apart from the provision for widows already mentioned, women could and did inherit property, even if it was only in default of a male heir. In 1757, Sarah Bank inherited two unnamed tenements and some land from her father, Peter Iredell; in 1718, Jane Head inherited Hill from her sister, Mary. Hannah Burnyeat (a Quaker; Friends were renowned for their fair treatment of women) was clearly a great heiress, owning land at High Iredale and High Nooke, and houses at Crabtreebeck and Thrushbank. When she married Jacob Fearon in 1728, this property of course technically passed to him as her husband and was recorded in the court rolls as an 'alienation', but it is noticeable that husband and wife became joint tenants to the property so Hannah presumably had a great deal of say in its running. There are a number of other instances of husband and wife being joint tenants, particularly in the second half of the eighteenth century; interestingly, several of these also involved Quakers. In addition, women were not debarred from holding office in the manor, though this could be a mixed blessing. In 1718-19, two women - 'Widdow Allason and Widdow Pearson' became 'sessors' - probably the most unpopular job in the manor because it involved assessing how much rates each person paid, according to the value of his or her property. In 1744, Ann Burnyeat was one of three constables in the Manor.

But back to Anthony Patrickson and his agreements. The 1698 Brackenthwaite agreement states very clearly that the Lord had no power to evict tenants unless they were guilty of 'treason, murder, manslaughter, rape, burglary, felony or petty larceny'; as not a lot of this went on in Loweswater, Brackenthwaite and Thackthwaite, tenants were fairly safe. But if anyone had any expectations of peace following the verdict in Chancery and the various agreements Anthony Patrickson made with his tenants, they were to be sadly disillusioned. Not all the tenants were happy with the detail of the Chancery verdict and some boycotted the payment of rents and fines (paid on the death of Lord or tenant). Patrickson himself seems to have decided to get round the judgement by whatever devious means he could think of, and the dispute dragged on through petty annoyances, the Courts and agreement after agreement, well into the next century. By this time the sins of the fathers were being visited on the sons and daughters. In 1632 for instance, Margaret Pearson ended up in prison in Carlisle for persistently complaining that she hadn't been allowed to take possession of the house at Peil left to her by her father, Matthew Robinson. This was not Anthony's fault, however; he had been dead five years and his son Henry - a real chip off the block where spending and deviousness were concerned - was Lord of the Manor. Despite the Patricksons' attempts to end the rules however, the system, as embodied in the 1598 Brackenthwaite agreement and others, and in the Manor Court, survived, more or less efficiently, for over 200 years after their time.

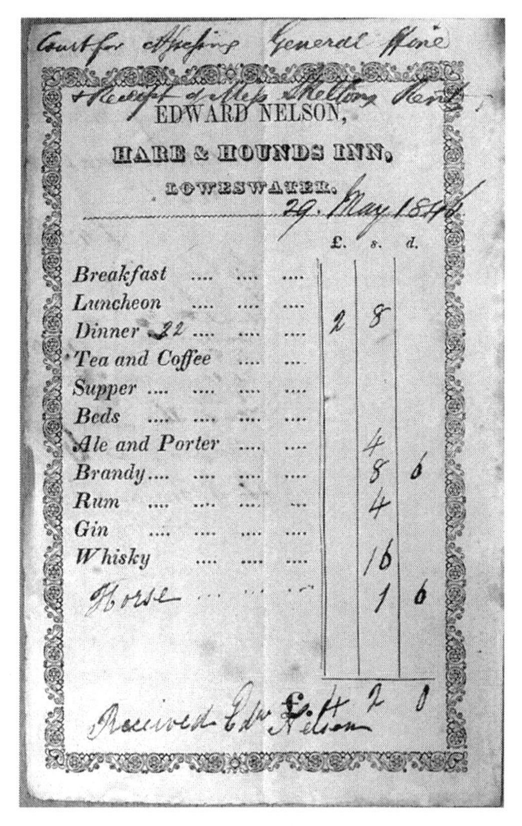

Court for Affeering General Fine
+ Receipt of [illegible] Rent

EDWARD NELSON,

HARE & HOUNDS INN,

LOWESWATER. 29. May 1845

	£.	s.	d.
Breakfast			
Luncheon			
Dinner 22	2	8	
Tea and Coffee			
Supper			
Beds			
Ale and Porter		4	
Brandy		8	6
Rum		4	
Gin			
Whisky		16	
Horse		1	6
	£4	2	0

Received Edw Nelson

The bill for the manor court held at the Hare and Hounds (Kirkstile) in May 1845, by permission of Waugh and Musgrave, Solicitors

CRIME AND PUNISHMENT[1]

In Cockermouth Castle are Manor Court Rolls which give a fascinating glimpse into medieval life in Loweswater until the early years of Henry VIII's reign. Much of this year must have been spent in routine farming tasks but when excitement of an illicit nature intervened, the culprits came before the Manor Court and the Rolls record their punishments.

Many of the crimes dealt with were social crimes, offences against the system in which the Lord of the Manor's permission was necessary for all kinds of everyday business. Unless you had a licence for instance, it was illegal to chop down timber even for the best of reasons; in 1535, James Dalton was fined for cutting down 'forbidden material for the rebuilding of three houses lately burnt down by a violent fire'. The common practice, however, was to cut first and pay the fine later; even Richard Robynson, the chaplain (Loweswater was then a chapel in the parish of St Bees) happily taking part. Also frequent was the rather odd offence of keeping 'foreign sheep' (that is, sheep belonging to another parish) on the common, including the case of a farmer summoned in 1517 for keeping *half* a foreign beast. (This was presumably a sheep owned by two separate people.)

There were millers summoned for damning a stream in the wrong place, thereby causing flooding in stormy weather, and for taking more corn tax than they were entitled to. (Millers were notorious for this last offence.) Farmers were summoned for 'narrowing the highway to the common nuisance' and for not keeping their homes in good repair. It was even illegal to play dice or to gather wool in the fields (no doubt because the wool technically belonged to the Lord of the Manor even when it was hanging in little tufts on the hedges).

The procedure of the court was to call a jury consisting of any number from 5 to 12 people depending on the size of the village involved. These were not to judge the innocence or guilt of the defendants but to bring the cases to court - more a police role. These jurymen were understandably not always popular with their fellow-villagers, encountered some resistance to their attempts to bring people to court and on occasion found themselves summoned for using undue force.

Fining was the most common penalty, 3 shillings and 4 pence, and six shillings and 8 pence being the favourite penalties - large sums in those days. On one occasion Jak [Jack] Newcom went home forty-one shillings the poorer, but he was a persistent offender, keeping dogs running wild, driving his neighbours' cattle off the common and fencing off part of the common when he had been told not to. He was also prone to suing his father and brother for debt; his brother generally retaliated in kind and sued Jak.

---

[1] First published December 1986.

When some more severe penalty was called for, the court faced a problem. Prisons in those days were not places of long-term punishment but merely temporary accommodation for those awaiting punishment; the court therefore could only 'remove' persistent offenders, that is, throw them out of the parish and let them thieve in some one else's jurisdiction. Offenders in Loweswater had to be removed from all the parishes under the Honour of Cockermouth which covered a surprisingly large area of West Cumberland and in practice people were frequently harboured by relatives and friends. In 1506, John and Christopher Jakson were fined sixpence each for harbouring their own wives, Issabill and Katarine. In 1520, the unnamed wife of Robert Jakson was ordered either to mend her ways or to be removed from the district; her crime was that she had a house on the common 'where she is suspected of harbouring low characters or thieves at divers times'. Since she was still in the valley some years later, she must have heeded the warning and behaved - or was too crafty to be found out again.

Not all the accused took their convictions in a philosophical spirit; many were the people fined sixpence for saying that the court had been less than fair. Richard Robynson, the chaplain, was rather more harshly dealt with when he made too much fuss over the court's decision about the disposal of the goods of Janet Wilkinson, recently drowned at Loweswater. He was fined six shillings and sixpence for 'wrongfully upbraiding ... and scolding the court'.

Sadly, the Court Rolls are incomplete and only tantalising references remain to what might have been the most interesting case of all, 'murder and felony viz the death of Robert Thomson' at Rannerdale in 1525. This was evidently a conspiracy and most of the culprits fled. One, Richard Newcom, however, remained in the valley and was 'harboured and entertained to the common hurt' by at least five of the local residents, including his father. These five were fined twenty pence each.

What happened to Richard Newcom afterwards is not recorded but one of his five accomplices suffered further. Infuriated by his conviction, 'Robert Hudson of Gaytescarth and his wife did cut down their gate in the highway upon the gate posts and carried the same gate into the water called Crombokwatter and they did throw it in'. For this wilful destruction of the Lord's property, Robert Hudson was fined twenty shillings, far more than they had been fined for harbouring a murderer. The court knew where its priorities lay.

BOUNDERS[1]

It's amazing how the simplest tasks can suddenly become terribly complicated. What, I thought, could be simpler than making a table of the population of Loweswater at various times in its history? Admittedly, the earlier part must be largely guesswork, based on formulae that local historians have worked out. For instance, it is estimated that in the 17th and 18th centuries there was an average of five persons per family; as there were 63 families based on the Hearth Tax list of 1664, there were at least 315 people in the parish. (There could have been more as some families might have been too poor to have a hearth to tax.) Likewise, the historian W. G. Hoskins recommends taking ten years' worth of baptisms in the registers, finding a yearly average and then multiplying the answer by 30 - the figures for 1626-32,[2] 1675-84 and 1700-1709 have been reached in this way.

Of course, problems could arise if the Vicar or parish clerk was lazy and forgot to enter all the births; is this the reason for the surprising drop in population from roughly 330 in the 1680s to only 240 in the first ten years of the next century? Perhaps, I thought, it would be wiser to turn to more reliable figures, such as those produced by the census taken (nearly) every ten years from 1801 onwards. At first glance, there seems to be no difficulties with these figures. Everything's explicable - that big jump in population between 1801 and 1820 is explained by the influx of workers for the lead mine at Netherclose and the drop between 1831 and 1851 is explained by the closure of the mine and the prompt departure of most of the miners. A close look, however, raises doubts.

Until 1881, population figures for Loweswater had always been given separately from those for Brackenthwaite which was in the chapelry of Lorton in the parish of Brigham. In 1886, however, parish boundaries were changed and Loweswater took in part of Brackenthwaite. Which means that it is difficult to compare the figure before 1886 with the figures afterwards which in turn makes it difficult to work out the rate of population rise or fall, the population per acre etc. All because of a small change in boundaries.

Tricky things, these boundaries. When, for instance, the parish registers talk of Thackthwaite, they mean only the hamlet as it exists today. When the Manor records talk about it they mean anything from Foulsyke to Hill. On the other hand, when the Manor records refer to Waterend, they mean the single site known by that name today; when the parish registers say Waterend, they mean Waterend, Place, Iredale Place, Jenkinson Place, High Iredale ... Neither provides a handy little map to tell you where Waterend finishes or Thackthwaite starts. You get the impression that no

[1] First published April-May 1989.

[2] This period covers only eight years owing to a break in the parish registers.

one was quite sure. Around the mid-19th century a ferocious dispute sprang up between the people of Mosser and the people of Loweswater (and their Lord of the Manor) as to where precisely was the boundary between the two townships. The problem was that in the 1830s much land on the fell between Loweswater and Mosser had been enclosed and there was an argument as to whether the walls were in the right place. The people of Mosser said that they'd always let their sheep roam as far as Crabtreebeck; the people of Loweswater said *you may have done but you should not have.* The end result was a court case which the people of Mosser lost to the tune of £250. According to a story current at the time (I've not yet been able to confirm or refute it) Mosser's counsel may not entirely have had his heart in the case; he was courting the daughter of Loweswater's Lord of the Manor.

Even at a personal level, boundaries were a source of contention. In 1742, William Woodville of Place and his neighbour, John Pattinson, quarrelled over a 'Markstone formerly set in the waste ground about the tofts'. Both were Quakers and Friends hurried to mediate; Philip Burnyeat (of Mosser) and Jonathan Harris were to 'investigate and enquire of neighbours' as to the rights and wrongs of the situation, and Samuel Robinson and Japeth Fletcher (of Mockerkin) were to arbitrate. As the quarrel does not appear in any other records, it is likely it was settled by the enquiry.

These were problems which could not be allowed to fester, of course, which is where bounders come in. These are not the sort of cads that Bertie Wooster would have understood by the term, but verbal maps designed to be walked. So, for those of you who are keen to combine exercise and a little practical do-it-yourself history, I hereby offer two bounders (and a prayer for fine weather). A good map is also recommended.

The first bounder - a mere stroll - comes from the Manor Court Rolls for 1746 and was clearly written down to resolve a dispute over where the common began and ended. Walkers should start from the foot of Scale Force. (The spelling and odd punctuation in both bounders comes from the originals.)

> *We present upon evidence, upon view of our owne knowledge that the boundary between Scale and the Common shall extend from the force foot as have marked the same on by the foot of Bleacrag to the force corner thereof and so up a green slack to a leavel a littal a Bove and from thence to extend forward to the Ruddabeck head in the most convenient place where a hedge may be lett and then on the leavell ... from thance through ...[?] Hen Howes to the middle of Blaidabeck or there a bouts and we think it proper ... that a sufficient hedge be Built by the owner of Skale in tow [sic] years time after the date hear of and John Hudson to endeavour to keep his sheep from there heath*

there in winter time between all saints and the 25 of March for the said two years.

The second Bounder - definitely a day's trip requiring strong footwear and warm clothing - was drawn up to delineate the boundaries of Loweswater and Thackthwaite and dates from 1576. (The original can be seen in the Cumbria Record Office in Carlisle Castle.) The words 'as even water dealeth' are a piece of legal jargon whose exact meaning is obscure, at least to me. Suggestions as to its meaning are welcomed.[1]

Item. They [the jury] say upon their oaths, that the Boundary of Loweswater and Thackthwaite Beginneth at the River of Cocker up the Mare-beck until Dry-gill-foot and so up Dry-gill-Borrom to Dry-gill-Head And from Dry-gill-Head to the Tarn of Hudsceth, and so as Even water dealeth unto the height of Smythy-fell and to the farm called Sower foot. And from thence as Even water dealeth to White Riddin-gill And so down the said Gill to the Dub-beck; And up Dub-beck to Bramley Carr. And so up Bramley-Carr to Meare-gill-foot. And so up Meare-gill to Meare-gill head. And so up as Even Water dealeth to a cross upon the Height of Bourne-bank. And from the Height of Bourne-bank as Even water dealeth to a Rock of Stones between West Gill-Head and Corn-gill-Head. And from the said Rock of Stones as Even water dealeth to the Man of Black-ffell. And from the Man of Black-ffell as Even water dealeth to the height of the White Stones and so as even water dealeth to the Brown Stealfoot and so up Brownsteal to the Height of Flowtron And so the height of the Scarr And to the Height of Starling Dod and so as Even Water dealeth to Gill-filter-Beck-head and so to High Steal Top and so as Even Water dealeth to the Three foot Brandrith and so from the Three foot Brandrith down to the Wterside called Warranskaile Beck and down the side of Buttermire Water to Buttermire Dubs, and so down the side of Crumacke Water to Cocker Head. And so down Cocker as the Meadows goeth until Mara-beck-foot aforesaid.

---

[1] A boundary placed 'as even water dealeth', or a similar form of words, just follows the watershed, usually a ridge. Ed.

Oh, I nearly forgot. Here are the population figures that started all this.

POPULATION OF LOWESWATER

1626-32	450	[data incomplete]
1664	315	[at least]
1675-84	330	
1700-10	240	
1801	294	
1811	336	
1821	440	
1831	454	
1841	436	
1851	391	
1861	392	
1871	372	
1881	315	
1891	388	
1901		[Unknown]
1911	288	
1921		[Unknown]
1931	262	
1941		[No census taken]
1951	219	
1961	174	
1971	202	

AS CLERKES FINDEN WRITTEN[1]

Although we know there was a chapel at Loweswater from about 1125 AD, no details remain of the earliest chaplains, or - as they were known in the Middle Ages - clerks (hence the line from the medieval carol quoted as title to this article), St Bees Priory, to which the Loweswater living then belonged, had only two chaplains to cover its enormous parish, and these must inevitably have been travelling men, visiting such remote chapelries as Loweswater only a few times a year. For the rest of the time, the parishioners must have had to read the services themselves. By 1548, however, St Bees had at least six curates and there is the first evidence that the Loweswater curate at least was resident in his chapelry.

1506 provides the first reference by name to a curate. Robert Wilkinson. A good Loweswater name, that - all the early clerks seem to have been local men ministering to the needs of a community they knew well. Perhaps Robert identified too closely with the community; like many of his parishioners, he cut down oak wood - for building, probably - without asking the permission of the Lord of the Manor. For that, like some of his parishioners, he was fined 2d.

And so Robert appears and disappears; I know of no other reference to him. Three years later, he was probably dead, as his place had been taken by a man called Richard Robinson.

Richard marks a special point in the history of the church at Loweswater, as he was the resident curate when Henry VIII decided to divorce Catherine of Aragon. Like many another cleric, he began as a Catholic, found himself entirely in agreement with Henry's comments about the Pope, and ended his days, probably in the reign of Edward V, Henry's son, as a devout protestant, apparently still in possession of his curacy.

He was evidently a man of strong opinions and no reticence when it came to expressing those opinions. In 1509, an 'inquisition' was set up to decide who should have the possessions of Jenet Wilkinson who had recently been drowned. Richard disagreed with the verdict and said so uncompromisingly, 'upbraiding the inquisition taken between parties and scolding against the said inquisition'. The Lord of the Manor took a dim view of all this and fined him 6s 8d.

In the aftermath of Henry VIII's divorce and the break with Rome, the ownership of Loweswater changed with bewildering rapidity, so bewildering that the exact sequence of events is not clear. Henry Percy, the 4th Earl of Northumberland and Lord of the Manor, tried to stave off bankruptcy (and suspicions of treasonable loyalties) by giving much of his land, including Loweswater, to Henry VIII. Henry, of course, turned a nice profit by selling off the property - to Richard Robinson, clerk.

---

[1] First published March 1992.

At least that's one version of events. It would have made Richard Lord of the Manor and would have been more expensive that a chaplain would be likely to afford even if, as suggested, he was in partnership with John Robinson of London, a goldsmith and, presumably, a relative. According to this version, the two men sold the property on again in the days of Queen Mary to Thomas Stanley, Esq.

Version II is, I think, a little more likely. This says that Richard in fact bought part of the land belonging to St Bees Priory (which by this time had been dissolved). This land was 'a cottage called Kirkstall [Kirkstyle?] and two little closes of land called Kirkcroft and Milnehow [Millhill].[1] Kirkstile, being so close to the chapel, could well have been Richard's home. At a later date, John Robinson (who, in view of Richard's changed loyalties might even have been Richard's son) sold the property to Thomas Stanley. Whatever the true version of events, Richard gained a little bit of immortality as it is generally accepted that he gave his name to Robinson Fell.[2]

After Richard's death, there seems to have been a gap in the orderly progression of curates. When the Bishop of the nearly-new diocese of Chester required details of his parishes in 1578, he was told that 'at Loweswater they have no servyse but as they provide themselves'. This neglect was general; at Lorton, for instance, the same document reports: 'The chancel is in very great decay'.

By 1592, however, Loweswater had a curate again - another local man, William Burnyeat. Like Robert Wilkinson, he too appears only fleetingly - as a signature put to the wills of two parishioners in 1592 and 1594. One of these wills would not be legal by today's standards; William witnessed the signing of the will of Peter Wilkinson, a young widower with a small son, even though he was a beneficiary, inheriting one white ... But there the will has become illegible with age.

Not much more is known of John Westray, who was curate by 1623. According to the will of Matthew Wilkinson of Waterend, John had been owed seven shillings by the deceased, part of a complicated and widespread network of debts designed to limit risks in bad years. Interestingly, John - unlike his predecessors and successors - was not literate; he made his mark on the will, rather like a large *O* joined to a small *n*.

---

[1] Kirkcroft was the name for the land where the school (now the Village Hall) was later built.

[2] In fact both versions are true in that Richard Robinson, formerly the Priest of the Chantry of St Michael in Brigham, obtained both the Lordship of the manors of Loweswater and Thackthwaite from the king in 1546, and in 1550 he purchased the land that had been taken from the priory in 1539, plus the manor of Brackenthwaite. Essentially this total is what was later owned by Patrickson. Ed

His successor, John Borranskail, was yet another local man, almost certainly related to William Borranskail, the curate at Lorton. A curious document from 1639 (signed upon the Feast Day of St Peter the Apostle) gives a different insight into the activities of a curate, this time as a mediator in disputes. It seems that there had been 'suits and controversies' between Thomas Robinson of Hie [High] House and John Iredell and his son William of High Iredell; John Borranskail and Charles Hudson were, by agreement between the parties, appointed to look into the problem and come to a decision which would then be binding on those concerned. The details of the dispute are difficult to disentangle from the resulting agreement, but it would appear that both sides owed each other money - the debts were to be cancelled out - and both were quarrelling over the ownership of certain fields, which Thomas Robinson said John Iredell had sold to him but which John Iredell said he had not. The arbitrators agreed with Thomas Robinson.

In 1673, after at least 40 years as chaplain, John retired and his place was taken by young Patricius Curwen. (It is not certain whether this was his baptismal name or a Latinised version of it - he always signed himself Patricius.) So young was Patrick that he was not fully ordained (he would therefore have been under 23 years old) and John, despite his retirement, continued to perform ceremonies such as baptisms, marriages and funerals, until Patrick was qualified to do so - about a year. John died in March 1674/5.

Curwen was a native of Lamplugh parish, born - so he writes in the parish registers - at Ribton Hall. His brother Anthony was the father of Elizabeth Pearson of Thrushbank (a widow) and, in 1690, was married for a second time, by Patrick at Loweswater, to a Distington woman. Patrick himself married a Loweswater girl, Barbara Fisher. They set up house at Gillerthwaite, where over the years seven children were born: John (1678); Christian (a daughter): 1680/81; Elianor (1683/84: died aged 2); Mary (1686); another Elianor (1688: died aged 1½); Christopher (1692) and Barbara (1694).

Curwen is the first curate of whom something like a personal portrait remains, although this description is in an official document and is merely answering set questions. It shows him performing duties which seem not very different in some respects from the duties of a modern-day vicar. 'He is constantly resident among us ... he reads morning and evening service, marriage, churching of women, burial of the dead and ... causes the Lord's supper to be celebrated yearly.' (Officially, it should have been celebrated at least three times a year.) A trace of religious controversy remains; the unknown writer is most insistent that Curwen has 'read the 39 Articles and declared his assent thereto.' Curwen 'refuses not to visit the sick or delay the baptism of infants in case of danger of death'. On a more personal note, the writer adds: 'He is a man of sober, reasonable and exemplary life' and thinks it worth remarking: 'He is of good conversation.'

(Also worth noting from this 1695 document is that Curwen not only had a 'convenient Seat wherein to read Divine Service' but also 'a pulpit with a decent cushion'.)

In 1700, Curwen moved from Loweswater – but not very far, merely moving to Lorton, where in 1707 he died, leaving 12d to each of his surviving children. After his tenure of office, the policy seems to have been to appoint as curates men from outside the parish. After him, too, records become more plentiful and it is relatively easy to document the lives of the Loweswater curates. But – oh to be able to fill in some of those 15th century gaps …

TAXING TIMES[1]

The end of the 17th century, like the end of the 20th, was a time when you were never quite sure what tax you would be paying next. There was even - on three occasions between 1660 and 1697 - a poll tax.

The problem faced by the government of the day was that the existing system of direct tax was bringing in less and less money. As this was payable on land worth 20/- per annum or on good worth £3, it's unlikely that many people in this area of the Lake District were wealthy enough to pay it anyway. So the hunt was on for new and better sources of income.

The Hearth Tax was rather more successful and lasted from 1662 until 1689. All households had to pay two shillings for every hearth in the house, unless they were exempt on grounds of poverty. Most families had one or two hearths; in Loweswater, out of 67 houses recorded, only three had two hearths, none had more.

The Hearth tax return for Loweswater survives in the Cumbria Record Office - unfortunately those people too poor to pay are omitted and those who are included are listed by name only. However, by comparing the list with the parish registers, it is possible to assign almost every name a house. It is obvious that the constables, who had the unenviable task of checking on their neighbour's honesty, started at Fangs, worked their way methodically down to the lake, round Kirkgate and the church area, along to Thackthwaite and then went back to Mockerkin and Sogill. The more prosperous families were those of John Wood at High Cross, Thomas Allason at Godferhead and Philipp Burnyeat, a Quaker, at Crabtreebeck.

The list also reveals that there must have been a fair amount of inbreeding, despite church ordinances. Half the households listed (33 out of 67) shared only six surnames: Iredale, Pearson, Mirehouse, Burnyeat, Wilkinson or Jackson. There were no less than thirteen families of Iredale alone and confusion is made worse by the fact that the number of first names used was also very small. Of the heads of Iredale families, four were called William (two at Fangs, one at High Nook), three were John and three Peter. One John lived at Kirkgate or possibly Stealbank; George was a weaver at Peill on the shores of Crummock Water. Henry lived at Godferhead next to the more prosperous Allasons. A whole cluster of Iredales lived at Thackthwaite - three Peters, two Johns and the last William. Sorting out whose children are whose in the parish registers is a nightmare.

So much for national taxes. In addition there were plenty of local ones, for instance, the highway rate - until 1691, residents of a parish had either to give labour when necessary to repair the roads or to give a cash

[1] First published July/August 1991.

payment in lieu. After 1691, the parish simply levied a rate on everyone and hired labourers with the money.

The most notorious local tax, however, was tithes, the tenth of yearly produce payable to the church and a source of endless argument between Anglicans and Quakers, the latter of whom believed that priests were at best useless and at worst evil and on no account should be given money.[1] Quaker refusal to pay tithes resulted in the unedifying spectacle of tax farmers raiding Quaker farms and appropriating sheep to pay the tithes. As far as wealthier Quakers like Philip Burnyeat and Anne Dixon (of Waterend) were concerned, this was a burden. For smaller farmers it could be a disaster; in 1622 for instance, Thomas Fletcher of Thrushbank lost a quarter of the lambs he had bred that year (3 out of 12). William Mirehouse in 1689 lost a sheep, 'he having but ten of the last year's breeding'. Crops were taken too; in 1692, John Read lost 30 stooks of bigg (barley) and 74 of oats worth in total £2 13s.

Quaker records being unusually complete, it is possible to deduce something of the size of Quaker farms and even of good and bad years. Anne Dixon of Waterend clearly had the largest flocks of Friends in Loweswater, regularly breeding 50-55 lambs a year. Phillip Burnyeat bred between 37 and 40. At Thrushbank, Thomas Fletcher had a smaller flock that his neighbour Peter Burnyeat; Thomas bred 16-19 lambs, Peter around 30. The breeding record for Peter can be reconstructed almost entirely between 1679 and 1687; 1682 was a bad year - he only had 25 lambs. 1684 was worse - he only had 17. The records for Phillip Burnyeat confirm this; his lambs in 1683 numbered 43, in 1684 only 28.

In addition to tithes, there were the church 'sesses' or rates, paid whenever the church needed repairs and usually amounting to fourpence to sixpence a household. Quakers refused to pay this too and regularly had household goods appropriated as a fine. Most seem to have been made of pewter - two pewter spoons worth one shilling were taken from Thomas Fletcher in 1690, a pewter sale 'seller' from James Dickinson of Mockerkin in 1678 and a pewter dish from James Dickinson in 1673. This latter was worth one shilling one penny, though the rate was only fourpence. James Dickinson claimed that the collectors - William Pearson of Fangs and Peter Bragg of Waterend - spent the difference on drink.

---

[1] The word tax is used loosely here in connection with tithes. Tithes were paid to the clergy as their living, being originally a tenth of the increase of living things. Lambs not ewes, corn less seedcorn, eggs etc. The church rate or sess was for the church building. The tithes of Loweswater were the property of St Bees priory until the dissolution when they were sold as private property to a lay impropriator who would choose and pay the Vicar of St Marys. By 1839 Loweswater tithes worth £65 were paid to Sir Francis Fletcher Vane of Armaside Hall. Quakers would pay neither church rates nor tithes. Ed

But by far the most important tax locally was the poor rate, levied to pay for the upkeep of the parish poor. Under an act of 1682, the poor were only to be 'relieved' in the parish in which they had a legal settlement i.e. in which they had been born, had lived for some years or served an apprenticeship, paid poor rate or served in a parish office. If you did not fall into any of these categories and became poor you could be removed to another parish and passed on like a parcel, until, possibly, like many of the poor, you died. It was vitally important, therefore, if you moved, to be able to prove your right to poor relief by obtaining a certificate to that effect from your parish of origin. Thus in 1735, Loweswater parish registers describe William Usher, a waller of Waterend, as 'a certificate man of the parish of Rosthwaite'.

No records of moneys collected for the poor and paid out to them in Loweswater survive, so the large number of people who must have been living below the poverty line are only remembered in isolated, sad entries in the parish registers. Many were poor because of age and inability to work. 'Ann Iredale of Waterend, widow, a pauper, aged 92 years' (buried 1740). 'Thomas Iredale, a poorman – it is said he dye'd [in a fall from] the back of a horse in ye lane rear of Loweswater church' (buried 1701). Robert Pearson of Fangs, 'a poor man maintained by the parish' (buried 1725). Others were outsiders, often wanderers. 'William Byer, a poor child left in the parish' (buried 1728/29). A year later, 'Dorothy Bolton, a poor traveller, buried'.

And finally – there were the 'smoake hens'. No, no relation to firedogs, but a tax so obscure that even the staff of the Archive Office in Carlisle hadn't hear of it. Evidently, you paid a hen to the owner of the tithes for the privilege of his allowing you to let smoke from your fire go up your own chimney. The 'best' description of it is from Quaker records again and dates from 1678. 'George Starts preist at Isell and Richard Peirson of Blindcrake in Isell Mannor Court for 9 years' Tythes, as 9 hens for his smoake passing nine years up his chimney'.

Richard in turn claimed that George Starke had come round and taken '12 pounds of yarn, a roasting knopp, a pann and 2 pewter dishes worth 12 shillings' which ought to have amply covered the value of the unpaid hens, valued each at about five pence. In 1684, Phillip Burnyeat had a cock (worth sixpence) appropriated and Peter Burnyeat a hen (worth five pence). Thomas Fletcher had no hens so he had to give up a pewter tankard worth one shilling and two pence. The manufacturers of pewterware must have made fortunes out of Quaker refusals to pay tithes and associated taxes.

Supposed portrait of George Fox, 1677, in *Quaker Meeting*, by Egbert Van Heemskerk.

Chapter 7: QUAKER COMMUNITY

These five articles are about Quakers, or Friends, and they are collected together separately because, as far as was practicable, Quakers formed a self-contained community, wishing to live according to their beliefs and principles without conflict with the mainstream, after the early evangelism. They formed a religious society during the commonwealth period after 1650. The temporary abolition of the monarchy and of the authority of bishops created a space in which new groups could form and compete for members, though they risked local opposition. Quakers rejected the religious authority of kings, bishops, popes and even books, believing that religious truth came in a spiritual and unmediated way to all people, including women; but moderated by the group, and taking as a starting point the Christian culture they all shared. Why Quakerism took root west of the Cocker is unknown and perhaps accidental, but Quakers needed to concentrate together to survive as a group, and the Pardshaw Meeting became one of the most successful. Pardshaw, Eaglesfield, Dean, Mosser Whinfell, and properties north and west of Loweswater Lake contained an increasing percentage of Quakers, who intermarried and kept their commercial relationships as much as possible within their community.

Grouping together for mutual support and protection became essential following the restoration of the established church and of the monarchy in 1663. The Quakers' threat was political, not religious, in that they refused, like Catholics, the religious authority of the reinstated bishops and of Charles II; who was not really a model of morality. The sufferings in which hundreds died in prison, many through civil actions for non-payment of tithes, lasted until the toleration of 1689 under William of Orange. The Quaker policy of non-violence and of recording and publishing the sufferings led to an acceptance that was not extended to Catholics and Unitarians. It also resulted in a large number of records being made and surviving, making Quaker family histories easiest to do. The priority necessarily given to educating and training the young, of both sexes, was important in giving Quakers strength in the developing commercial and industrial society of the eighteenth century. If weaver's son John Dalton, of Eaglesfield, had not been a Quaker's son, then probably his occupation would have been weaving rather than developing atomic theory.

In Loweswater the two groups co-existed socially and co-operated where it was necessary, in say the manor court. But Quakers were in the Pardshaw Meeting first and Loweswater Township second, and the tensions come through in the articles. Robert Southey (no relation), in the persona of a visiting Spaniard, also wrote an affectionate but quizzical portrait of Quakers in 1807, and he was also familiar with Loweswater.[1]

[1] Southey, Robert 1807. pp. 349-359 (Cresset Press Edition 1851)

FRIENDS AND NEIGHBOURS[1]

In 1753, Joseph Besse published a book with one of the snappy titles so beloved of the time. The book was called *A collection of the Sufferings of the people called Quakers for the Testimony and a Good Conscience from the Time of their being first distinguished by that Name in the Year 1650 to the Time of the Act commonly called the Act of Toleration, granted to Protestant Dissenters in the first Year of the Reign of King William and the Third of Queen Mary in the Year 1689.* Joseph Besse had gathered together all the information he could find concerning the legal penalties exacted from Quakers in the first 39 years of their existence - each county has a section of its own, revealing how a national struggle affected individuals.

To the government, any challenge to the Church was a challenge to the State as the two were officially one. To admit yourself a Quaker was to court trouble even if you broke no laws. Thus 1661 was an uncomfortable year for John Dixon of Waterend. In February he wrote a letter to Hugh Tickell of Portinscale asking him to send money collected for the poor to London, for Friends there to distribute. Unfortunately, as John walked home from Cockermouth one day, he dropped the letter on the road and it was picked up and handed to the authorities.

John was arrested and closely questioned by two local justices. He managed to convince them that Friends were 'as harmless and innocent people as they pretend to be', but they still wrote to London to express their opposition to Quakers. 'Their continued meetings amongst them and sending many of their faction to ... all parts beyond the sea, and maintaining them; (if permitted) may give to[o] great an opportunity to malicious dissatisfied spirits through such like pretences to effect their dangerous designes to ye prejudice of the present Government'. In short, better that a few innocent men are arrested and sent to the Assizes than leave a loophole which dangerous men may exploit. The times, after all, were unsettled; Charles II had recovered his throne only the previous year and still felt insecure. John Dixon, described later by the Governor of Carlisle as being 'troubled with the evil', was sent to prison. Not for the first time; his first arrest had taken place only three years after George Fox's arrival in Cumberland.

Joseph Besse's book details the ways Quakers could get into trouble. Of these, refusing to pay tithes for the upkeep of the Church, is the best-known: Quakers believed that each individual could speak directly to God and that therefore there was no need for a Priesthood or Church. Other offences included refusing to swear - that is, to take an oath. Punishment, at least for a first offence, was generally a fine; thus a man in Uldale was fined £2 10s for refusing to produce a witness to swear that his wife had

[1] First published August-September 1989.

been buried in a woollen shroud. Quakers said that to swear that they were telling the truth was tantamount to suggesting that the rest of the time they were prone to telling lies. John Tiffin of Mockerkin was one of several men fined in 1663 for refusing to swear; Philip Burnyeat of Thrushbank was also fined in the same year - twenty shillings.

If the fines were not paid, 'distresses' could be made, that is, goods could be seized and sold to pay the fine. In the case of tithes, goods could be seized to the value of the payment due. After John Dixon's death in 1679, livestock was taken every year from his widow's fields in lieu of the tithes she wouldn't pay: 5 lambs in 1680, 9 lambs worth £1 2s 6d in 1681, 7 sheep in 1682 and so on. What was taken was often worth more than the tithes due and sometimes it was all the Friend possessed: a record of 1679 states that Anne lost 8 young sheep 'being all she had'.

Other injustices in the system have a curiously modern ring. Parents could be made to pay fines incurred by their children. 'Masters for their servants,' Besse says 'and even such as being themselves Conformists, had servants or others in their families who were not'. Because of this and the fact that those were churchgoers had to pay more for such things as church repairs because Quakers would pay nothing, it is no surprise to find that Quakers could be unpopular with their neighbours. There was no shortage of people willing to exercise their right to seize Quaker property; in 1681, for instance, 'came Thomas Wilkinson and John Mirehouse both of Miresyke in Loweswater and took from Thomas Fletcher of Thrushbank in Loweswater one little can with a wooden dish for the bell-house Sesse [a rate levied for repairs to the church] Value 5d'.

Sometimes, however, neighbours could be supportive and refuse to buy goods distained from Quakers, as seems to have happened in 1683 at Pardshaw Cragg. On this occasion the gesture seems to have misfired. Local justices broke up a meeting at the Cragg at which Peter Fearon of Mockerkin was speaking. A fine of twenty shillings was imposed on Peter and several others for unlawful assembly. Peter asked that he should be allowed to pay the entire fine himself as he could afford it and the others could not; the justices refused. Five men, including Peter and John Tiffin, had goods taken to pay the fine, amongst the goods being an obviously excellent horse valued at £3. The total value of property taken was £17 19s.

Besse relates what happened next. 'When the Goods were exposed to Sale, and Buyers of them could not be found, the Justice ordered his own Servants to purchase some of them, which they did at a very low price, and the Officers, to supply the Defect [i.e. the rest of the fine] made another Seizure on some of the persons concerned'.

For persistent offenders, there was the threat of imprisonment. For John Pattinson of Waterend in 1664, it was the last step in a long process, after prosecution in the church courts for non-payment of fines, and excommunication. For some it was a recurring experience; John Burnyeat of

Crabtreebeck served a number of sentences, as did John Dixon. It was not unknown for women to give birth in prison, or for elderly Friends to die there.

Most frequently, imprisonment was imposed on those who publicly contradicted priests, though Besse does not record any incidents at Loweswater Church and it may be that the Vicar there was quietly sympathetic. The Vicar of Dean did not get off so lightly; perhaps he had commented too strongly on the habit of Quakers meeting in his parish at Pardshaw.

There was a very old custom, and a legal right, for any member of the congregation to speak in Church after the Minister had finished; Friends took advantage of this custom to ask some awkward questions or even to deny the truth of what the Priest had said. In 1654, for instance, John Head of Mockerkin delivered 'some queries to the Priest of Deane at his own House' (i.e. the church) and Peter Head [his brother?] testified 'to the truth in the same place'. John served two months and Peter fourteen weeks 'in a close Room amongst Felons in the Heat of Summer'. In 1685, a proclamation was issued, warning Quakers not to take advantage of this custom; the proclamation made no difference – in 1657, John Burnyeat was amongst five men imprisoned at Carlisle (in his case for 23 weeks) for 'reproving the Priests at several Times and Places'.

This was harsh treatment but the authorities had some cause to worry for order and law. Friends' habits of standing up to preach in Church frequently provoked anger and anger often turned to violence, as at Dean in 1654.

The chief person involved in this incident was a Friend called Thomas Stubbs. 'Thomas Stubbs,' Besse says, 'was concerned to go into the steeple-house at Deane, where, when the Priest had done, he said: Thou daubest the People up with untempered Mortar; whereupon the Priest bid his Hearers fight for the Gospel; they fell violently upon Stubbs and some of his Friends, tore their clothes and beat them cruelly. The Priest's son in particular sorely bruised the face of Richard Richardson. After which, two Justices sent Stubbs to prison.'

The Justices, however, seem to have been sympathetic to Stubbs, perhaps feeling that the Priest's response had been unreasonably oppressive. Consequently, they wrote Stubb's discharge from prison on the same piece of paper as his commitment to prison, clearly intending that he should be released at once. Unfortunately, the gaoler demanded the fees he would normally be paid to commit a prisoner and to release him, and Stubbs remained in prison for fourteen weeks until either the fine was paid or the gaoler decided he wasn't going to receive it.

Finally, King William and Queen Mary decided that Friends were no real danger to the state after all and passed the Toleration Act abolishing penalties for such things as refusing to pay tithes, swear and oath and so on.

Besse estimates that in the preceding ten years, goods to the value of £2215 15s 9d were taken from Quakers in Cumberland in lieu of the tithes they wouldn't pay. He doesn't estimate the total length of time spent in prison by Friends, and the resentment of friends and neighbours is too intangible to measure but must have been all too tangible to face.

Friends Meeting House, Pardshaw, 1980s

EXCELLED BY FEW[1]

Loweswater has produced only one man famous enough to feature in history books and nowadays even he is little known. Yet in his own time, he was one of the best known Quakers and an enthusiastic missionary.

John Burnyeat was born at Crabtreebeck in 1632 and was baptised on 17 March. The parish registers supply all that is known of his early life. He was the son of Peter Burnyeat, a farmer, and had an older sister, Annas (born 1628) and an older brother (born 1629) who was also called John and who presumably died before the younger John's birth. Until 1653, John seems to have been happy farming, though he does record in later writings that he was uneasy spiritually. In that year, however, George Fox visited Cumberland and John was quickly converted to Quakerism.

At first he seems to have been content to attend Quaker meetings, but then a sense that he was not doing all that he could began to take hold of him. He felt that he should be converting other people to Quakerism and in 1657, four years after his own conversion, chose Aspatria as the place for his first missionary efforts.

The occasion was not entirely successful. He went to the 'steeple-house', heard what he thought was an extremely bad sermon from the Preacher and after the service himself started to preach in the churchyard. The churchgoers were hostile and threatening, and in some fear he decided to give up. But halfway home he felt ashamed and went back again. The preacher was just giving his afternoon sermon; John Burnyeat heard him in silence then got up in the church and preached back.

That time he seems to have got away unharmed. Doing the same thing a few weeks later he was beaten up, then arrested for being a dissenter and sentenced to twenty-three weeks in Carlisle gaol.[2] It was not the last prison sentence he served.

He was twenty-seven years old. During the next twenty-six years he travelled as widely as any of the early Friends, visiting mainly Scotland and Ireland. Everywhere he found both converts and enemies. In 1632 he was back in prison again - this time in Ripon, where he visited Friends imprisoned there. He stood up to say a few encouraging words and was promptly arrested by the gaoler. He was there for four weeks and defiantly held a meeting for worship every day. He ended up in solitary confinement. Next door to the gaol was a bowling alley where the magistrates enjoyed a game or two - Burnyeat climbed up to a window overlooking the alley and preached loudly to them. They were not appreciative.

---

[1] First published June/July 1987.

[2] John Burnyeat's encounters before gaol involved Lorton, Loweswater and Brigham. These extracts from his 'life' are included after this article. Ed.

Even out of prison, the conditions he endured were not pleasant. He travelled frequently in Ireland which was still largely unexplored and wild and dangerous countryside. Then in 1664 he crossed to the even less explored wastes of America, spending three years there. After a short break in England (and two spells in prison) he went back to America in 1671. Here people were more interested and less inclined to imprison Quakers though there was some persecution. His most enthusiastic audiences seem to have been Indians.

In 1683, he married an Irish Friend and settled in Dublin, serving another short prison sentence shortly afterwards. His son, Jonathan, was born in 1686 but sadly his wife died in 1688. Two years later, Burnyeat himself was dead of a fever that lasted twelve days.

Hutchinson, who wrote a *History of Cumberland* in 1794, described Burnyeat as 'a person well qualified for disseminating the principles and practices of ... Quakers ... who had been excelled by few in the pains he took in travelling in the service of the gospel'. His writings were many, though not particularly well-written, but many people treasured them for the reminders of a man well-loved whose 'gospel labours commanded reverence, being in doctrine clear, elegant and pathetic' (in the old sense of producing sympathetic emotions).

A postscript - his son, four years old at the time of Burnyeat's death, was sent back to his paternal relations in Cumberland, and at the age of twelve followed in his father's footsteps, travelling into Scotland as a missionary. He died, still travelling for Quakerism, at the age of twenty-two.

Truth Exalted

IN THE

WRITINGS

OF THAT

Eminent and Faithful Servant

of CHRIST

John Burnyeat,

COLLECTED

Into this Enſuing Volume as a *MEMORIAL* to his Faithful Labours in and ſor the *TRUTH*.

Prov. 10. 7. *The Memory of the Juſt is Bleſſed.*
Pſal. 112. 6. *The Righteous ſhall be had in Everlaſting Remembrance.*

LONDON:
Printed for Thomas Northcott in *George-Yard* in *Lumbard-Street.* 1691.

Title page from the writings of John Burnyeat, published 1691

John Burnyeat in Loweswater, 1657:- from pp. 23-25 of 'Truth Exalted'

... Then some time after I was moved by the Spirit of the Lord to go to Lorton, to speak to one Fogoe a Priest, who was preaching to the People in their Worship-house, and I stayed till he had done; and there he did affirm in his preaching to the People, that both he and they was without the Life of both the Law and the Gospel. And then I spoke to him, and questioned him what he had to preach, or to pray, that was without the Life of both Law and Gospel? But after a few words, he fell into a rage, and stirred up the People, and they fell upon me, and haled me out of the House, and did beat me, and the Priest did threaten to put me in the Stocks. So I came away; and that day two Weeks I was moved to go again to speak to the same Priest at Louswater, the Parish where I did then dwell; and when I came in, the People beginning to look at me, and take notice, the Priest bid them let me alone, if I would be quiet, he would discourse with me, when he had done. So I stood still and quiet, waiting upon the Lord; the Priest he prepared to go to Prayer, but when he saw that I did not put off my Hat (for I could not so do, because I could not joyn with him in his dead lifeless Prayers) Then instead of going to Prayer, he fell a railing against me, and said I should not stand there in that posture. At last I spoke to him, and did ask him, What he had to pray with, that was without the Life of both Law and Gospel. But he continued calling out to the People, to take me away; so that at last, my Father being there, and displeased with me for troubling their Minister, came himself and haled me out of the House, and was very angry with me. Then I stayed in the Grave-yard, till the Priest and People came out, and then I got to him, and spoke to him again, but he soon began to be in a rage, and to threaten me with the Stocks, and got away. And then I cleared my Conscience to the People of what I had to say, and so came away in great peace with the Lord.

Then not long after, in the same Year, I was moved of the Lord by his Spirit to go to Brigham, to speak to one Priest Denton, who then was preaching in the Steeple-house to the People; who in his Sermon, which he had before hand prepared, had many false Accusations, Lyes, and Slanders against Friends, and the Principles of the Truth. I stayed till he had done, and then did speak to him, but got little Answer; but immediately some of his Hearers fell upon me, and did beat me with their Bibles, and with a Staff, or Staffs, all along out of the House, and also out of the Grave-yard, that the next day I was sore with the Blows, and so the Priest commanded the Constable to secure me, and a Friend that was with me, and next day did cause him to carry us to Lancelot Fletcher of Talantyre, who did order a Warrant to be written for us, and so sent us from Constable to Constable, to the common Goal in Carlisle, where I was Prisoner three and twenty Weeks. And when I wrote a Paper to the Priest, wherein I answered his false Accusation, and sent it to him by a Friend, he would not read it, but, as I was told, put it in the fire and burnt it. ...

THE LETTER AND THE LAW[1]

With hindsight, John Dixon of Waterend probably felt that it had been foolish to carry a letter with sensitive comments in his pocket, but to do him justice, he had not really considered that the letter *was* sensitive. Perhaps he had been rather naïve.

His problem was that the political situation in 1661 was a bit sensitive too. Charles II, only a year back on his throne, was still feeling distinctly shakey and so were his ministers of state. The merest hint of a conspiracy against the king as leapt on as evidence that the spirit of Cromwell and the Commonwealth was not yet dead. Charles did not want to end on the executioner's black as had his father.

John Dixon was almost certainly a loyal subject of the king but he was certainly not a loyal supporter of the Church of England. He was a Quaker and religious unorthodoxy was considered tantamount of political treason. John had already been arrested several times, found himself in Carlisle gaol and then had been forced to travel, at his own expense, to London to answer questions there. His property had been confiscated to pay fines and tithes; in 1657, he and his wife Ann were so distressed at the persecution against them that they considered emigrating to America.[2]

Something persuaded them to stay however, and by 1661 they were at home in Loweswater, spending what time they could spare from farming and their young family in fund-raising.

Early in February 1661, John Dixon attended a meeting in Pardshaw which discussed what to do with money collected locally. He was given the task of writing to Hugh Tickell of Portinscale who was holding the money for safety. On 3 February, John wrote:

> *Deare friend, my deare love salutes thee and thy wife with the rest of thy family. This is to certify thee of our pseedings [proceedings] at ye Month Meeting you are desired to send your collection yt was for London with speed [and] you must send that which is for our own country service and it is ordered that there is a collection this month for ye servis of the truth to be brought in to the next month meeting att Quartell Hill at Thos Porters.*
> *Your friend in the measure of the Truth. John Dixon.*

[1] First published September 1992.

[2] See *A Place of Woodville's own* for the story of the marriage of Ann and John Dixon and *Friends and Neighbours* for the sufferings of Ann after John's death. The latter also gives an abbreviated version of this incident.

John put the finished letter in his pocket, and, for a reason unknown, set off to Cockermouth. Somewhere close to the town, the letter dropped out of his pocket.

At this point, the sequence of events can only be guessed, though with some degree of confidence. Some loyal Anglican found the letter, read the contents rather than forward it to Hugh Tickell, and immediately jumped to the conclusion that this involved a plot against the king. The letter was forwards to the nearest local Justices, Mr Lamplugh and Mr Tolson.

> *'This letter from one Quaker to another,' Mr Lamplugh wrote in alarm to Joseph Williamson Esq. at Whitehall (presumably a civil servant) 'contains suspicious expressions within this juncture of time where there is a discoverie of plottings and a suspicion of the actings thereof against the present Government in most parts throughout his majesty's] three kingdoms'.*

The Justices were most concerned at the mention of 'Meetings' and the suggestion of contact with Englishmen abroad. There was a tendency to believe that no Englishman would actually choose to live abroad and could only be doing so because of a 'disagreement' with the government; therefore every Englishman abroad was potentially a conspirator against that government. Mr Lamplugh, who was plainly not a foolish man, was inclined to think John Dixon harmless, but he was worried about infiltrators. He wrote:

> *Admitt their explanacion thereof to be truth and they as harmlesse and innocent people as they pretend to bee, yet their continued meetings amongst them and sending many of their faction to … all parts beyond the sea and maintaining them; [if permitted] may give to[o] great an opportunity to malicious dissatisfied spirits through such like pretences to effect their dangerous designes to yet purdice [prejudice] of the present government.*

In short, fake Quaker meetings might spring up around the country as fronts for treasonable plots.

Mr Williamson of Whitehall recommended that John Dixon should be arrested and questioned. So, in June 1661, John Dixon and Hugh Tickell were taken to Cockermouth where Messrs Lamplugh and Tolson questioned them. Details of the questions asked Tickell do not appear to have survived, but John Dixon's interrogation remains in State Papers.

He was first asked: 'What is the meaning of "Monthly Meeting"?'

He replied that the meeting was 'to know which poor need relief or are in prison, &c,' making it clear that he was not referring to Meeting for Worship but to the men's preparatory meeting.

'What is this collection for London?' This, John Dixon said, was destined for 'the relief of friends in Barbados.' The Justices wanted to know why these Friends were abroad; Dixon said that they were there 'to deliver the truth' - that is, they were missionaries.

Next, the two Justices queried Dixon about the 'collection for this country's service'. Dixon, it transpired, was using the word 'country' as we would use 'county'. He said the money was for the relief of the poor in Cumberland and for those in prison.

The Justices, you might expect, would have been interested in obtaining names of other people involved in this 'conspiracy' but the questions show that they barely bothered to ask. They queried how many were at the monthly meetings (about 10, John said) but then they left the subject. In all probability, such conscientious Justices probably had a good idea of the people involved; after all, priests kept track of people who failed to attend divine service, as the Quakers did. Instead of pressing for names, they went back to the question of the money and where it had gone.

John did not know exactly how much money had been raised, except that when the money for London had been sent off, forty shillings remained for the poor in Cumberland. The London money had been sent to one Gerard Roberts in London - he didn't know where Roberts lived. John had himself distributed the forty shillings to 'necessitous' persons, some in prison in Carlisle.

Which is exactly where John ended up.

It would be nice if this story had a triumphant ending, with John vindicated, or even a tragic ending such as John obstinately lingering in prison for his principles. In fact, it has no real ending at all, because, with a fine sense of anti-climax, the Justices lost interest in John and he was eventually released. He went home to Waterend where he lived with his wife and children, carrying on exactly as before, raising money for the poor in Cumberland and Quaker Friends in Barbados.

Though, as far as I'm aware, he never again lost any sensitive letters.

EXILES[1]

I came across Sarah Dixon in London in the records of the Society of Friends (Quakers). A small entry said: 'Sarah Dixon, daughter of Jonathan and Jane Dixon of Waterend in the Parish of Loweswater married Joseph Rooke of Newcastle-upon-Tyne at Pardshaw Hall, 1806 10 mo 22'.[2]

The Dixons were one of ten or twelve families living at Waterend; a Dixon had lived there since at least 1627. In the 18th century, Waterend was a firm stronghold of Quakerism, the Woodvilles, Pattinsons, Nutts, Jenkinsons, Wilkinsons, Johnsons, and Dixons all being firm adherents. In fact, Quakerism spread all down the Loweswater valley from Pardshaw, embracing several families in Mockerkin, one at Fangs, seven at Waterend and the families living at Crabtreebeck and Thrushbank. Curiously, in the rest of the parish, only one other family, of Iredells at Thackthwaite, were Quakers.

The Dixons had been Quakers since 1660 - very early considering that George Fox had only visited the area in 1653. Sarah was a fifth generation Quaker. What intrigued me was her marriage to someone from so far away. How had she met her husband? Were links between Cumbrian and Northumbrian Friends extensive?

Directories in Newcastle Central Library gave an address for the Rookes. Joseph was a linen or woollen draper and lived at 21 Dean Street. This is some distance from the modern centre of the city but in those days Newcastle was based around the Quayside and naval business, not far from Joseph's shop. It was to this address that Sarah and Joseph, both aged 30, came on their marriage in 1806.

Almost immediately Sarah was plunged into the affairs of the Society of Friends who were just building a new bigger Meeting House in Pilgrim Street. The records of the Women's Preparative Meeting mention her name only four months after her marriage; on a large number of occasions she was nominated as the women's representative to the Monthly (business) Meetings. At the same time, she was busy raising a family, giving birth to her first daughter, Marian (sometimes called Mary Ann) only ten months after her marriage. The following year another daughter, Jane, was born but died only eleven months later. Over the first nine years of her marriage, Sarah gave birth to five daughters, the others being Sarah (born 1810), another Jane (born 1814) and Elizabeth (born 1816, who died only three days before her first birthday).

Meanwhile the business seemed to continue without too many problems. Very few records remain - the newspapers mention only the

---

[1] First published August/September 1988.

[2] 22nd October 1806. Quakers did not use the names of the months, which they regarded as pagan in origin, but used numbers instead; Sarah's marriage, therefore, took place on the 22nd of the 10th month i.e. October.

more sensational events. Thus the Newcastle Courant records on Saturday, 21st October 1815 under deaths: 'On Wednesday last, Mr William Forsyth, shopman to Messrs Rooke and Co., drapers in Dean Street in this town. He fell down dead while opening the shop'. And on Saturday, 20 February 1819: 'Feb. 12, Friday, aged 41 [died] Mr Joseph Rooke of Dean Street ... Woollen draper, greatly respected and regretted'.

Nowhere is there a record of how Joseph died. His death caused immediate problems for Sarah, left as she was with three young daughters aged 12, 9 and 5. Friends came to her help and Rooke and Co became Bragg and Rooke with the aid of Charles Bragg, a Quaker draper in Pilgrim Street. Sarah and her daughters continued to live over the shop and to run the business. They diversified into selling hats and there is no sign that the business, although small, ran into any serious financial problems.

Throughout her marriage, it is likely that Sarah kept contact with her family in Loweswater. In the records of Newcastle meeting for 1819, Jane Dixon is recorded as coming to the Meeting from Pardshaw and it may well be that Jane was a relative of Sarah's (possibly her mother or sister) come to keep her company. Jane however died in 1821 and Sarah seems to have managed thereafter with the help of her growing daughters. The eldest, Marian, was also very active in the affairs of the Society becoming Clerk to the Women's Preparative Meeting in 1838. Sarah herself continued her Quaker activities certainly up to 1844, only five years before her death. On 15 February 1839, aged 62, Sarah died and was buried in the Friends Meeting House Burial Ground. Such is the efficiency of Friends' records that even the name of the gravedigger is preserved.

Sarah's three daughters, all in their mid twenties and early thirties, and all unmarried, continued to live in Newcastle for another eight or nine years. But it is clear that they still had contact with Loweswater. On Marian's death in 1846, the Annual Monitor, which recorded all Quaker deaths, wrote:

> *In the summer preceding her death, she spent some months in the Vale of Lorton near Pardshaw, for the benefit of the change of air. Many were the conflicts of flesh and spirit which she had then to endure, yet on her deathbed she acknowledge that in solitary places in the garden and in the fields, as well as at other times, she was often favoured with sweet spiritual refreshment whilst in retirement before God; and her countenance often indicated to those around her, the sweet serenity of her spirit.*

She was 38 years old and was buried near her mother.

The other two daughters, Sarah and Jane, remained in Newcastle only two more years, then Friends' records show that they both transferred to Pardshaw Meeting on 23 March 1848. The census of 1851 shows the

Dixons still living at Waterend though no Rookes are in the parish; it is of course possible that Sarah and Jane married in the three years between their return and the census.

The Quaker records (available in the Tyne and Wear Archive, Newcastle) solve one last puzzle; how did Sarah Dixon from Loweswater meet Joseph Rooke from Newcastle? It transpires that Joseph only became a member of Newcastle friends in 1797, having transferred from Pardshaw. In short, he was Cumbrian too. Pardshaw meeting covered a wide area, attracting Quakers from Cockermouth, Greysouthern, and even Whitehaven, so it is not clear where Joseph originated, but it is possible that he met Sarah on one of his visits home or that he knew her before he left for Newcastle.

Even a quick glance at Newcastle's list of members shows that Joseph and Sarah were not unusual in 'emigrating' from Cumberland to Newcastle. Jonathan Drewery, for instance, from Cockermouth, went as apprentice to his uncle at the age of sixteen, later married Ann Hudson from Setmurthy and raised his family in Newcastle. From the area covered by Pardshaw Meeting went also Christopher Robinson (1806), William Hall (1812), and Henry Bragg (1817). Women went too, apparently alone but sure of the support available from the Society - Hannah Fisher travelled to Newcastle in 1801. It seems that many young people looked to Newcastle to provide a better future than the depressed agricultural districts of Cumberland; in time of war (the French Revolution and the Napoleonic Wars) a port may have seemed to offer a better opportunity to make good. Sarah and Joseph never made their fortunes - although they seem to have survived quite comfortably - but it seems that the family never quite put down roots and that Sarah's last two surviving daughters returned 'home' to Cumberland.

WOMEN OF CONSCIENCE[1]

A while ago, while looking through documents connected with Pardshaw Quaker meetings, I came across a small leatherbound book containing a list of nine women's names. Each name was followed by a paragraph testifying against the payment of tithes. A typical entry, for instance, was under the name of Hannah Burnyeat.

> *I am in some measure a witness that Christ is come who put an end to the first priesthood that received tithes.*

A second woman, Mary Wilkinson, says:

> *It is my firm belief that … there is noe tithes due, but those that are found in the payment of it are denying the coming of Christ.*

Friends objected to paying tithes for the upkeep of the Church, on the grounds that there was no need for a Church or priesthood - each individual could speak directly to God. Tithes were paid by householders, generally, of course, men, so this list of nine women is distinctly unusual.

The list, unfortunately, has one big drawback - it is undated.

Never one to shirk a challenge, I wondered if it might be possible to date it. Obviously, judging by the handwriting and by the fact that it dealt with the controversy over tithes, it must date from the late 17th or early 18th centuries. But could it be dated more exactly?

Glancing over the list, I came across one familiar name, that of Ann Dixon. The Dixons lived at Waterend in Loweswater. John Dixon and his wife Ann were amongst George Fox's earliest converts in Cumberland; only three years after Fox's first appearance in the area in 1653, John was imprisoned for speaking against local priests. The couple considering emigrating to America but decided in the end to stay; they rebuilt their house at Waterend, Ann gave birth to two sons and John continued to be fined and imprisoned.

After John's death in 1679, Ann suffered yearly distraints of livestock in lieu of the tithes she would not pay, until William and Mary's Toleration Act of 1689 removed such penalties. For instance, in 1679, eight lambs were taken from her fields 'being all she had'; in 1680 she lost five more, in 1681 nine more and so on.

As was common in those days, John and Ann named their elder son John and he married the oldest daughter of the Woodvilles who lived just across the fields at the head of Loweswater lake, at what is now known as the Place. His bride, confusingly, was also called Ann. The marriage was

---

[1] First published November 1994.

controversial as the couple were too closely related (John's aunt was Ann's grandmother) and they ran off to Cockermouth to be married 'by a priest'. Friends in Pardshaw disowned John but he and Ann had guessed correctly when they assumed that, presented with a *fait accomplis*, Quakers would let the marriage stand. John apologised, was received back into the Society and Ann and the children were all staunch Quakers.

Which Ann did the document refer to? Both became widows at a fairly early age and ran the farm at Waterend for some years; both were therefore tithepayers at various times and would qualify to be on the list.

I started to investigate the other women on the list. The first name – that of Hannah Burnyeat – seemed most promising. I knew of only two Hannah Burnyeats, mother and daughter, and the elder had died before her husband, John Burnyeat of Crabtreebeck on the edge of Loweswater lake. I needed therefore to trace the younger Hannah, born in 1702.

By one of those strokes of luck that (all too rarely) happen, I stumbled across a reference to Hannah from 1729 while reading manor court records.

> *Hannah Burnyeat has alienated a tenement at High Iredale of 3s 4d rent … a parcel of a tenement of 1s 6d rent, a messuage and tenement at High Nooke of 15s 4d rent, a tenement at High Iredale at 1s 2d rent, a messuage and tenement at Crabtreebeck at 6s 8d rent, a parcel called Low and High Dub Ing of 1s 2d rent, a messuage and tenement at Thrushbank of 12s 7½d rent to the use and behoof of Jacob Fearon her intended husband for the terme of his Natural life and to the use of her the said Hannah and after the death of the longer lived of them then to the heirs of the said Hannah Burnyeat according to the customs of the Manor.*

A search of Quaker registers at Friends House in London revealed a family tragedy. After the death of her mother, Hannah's father had remarried but the second marriage was childless. The heir was Hannah's elder brother, Philip, but in 1725, Hannah's father John and Philip died within 16 days of each other. At the age of 23, Hannah inherited her father's considerable wealth.

All this helped to date the book roughly. The list must have been made after 1725 when Hannah, as a householder, became liable to pay tithes and before 1729 when she married and her husband took over that responsibility. The Ann Dixon of the document was clearly the younger Ann, who in 1725 would have been a widow of two years, aged 56.

By this time, I was hooked. Could I identify all the women on the list who had come together, perhaps at the little meeting house high on the fells at Pardshaw, to make a statement of their principles? Could I date the book exactly?

One or two of the other women were easy to identify once an approximate date was available. Esther Burnyeat, for instance, was Hannah's elderly cousin by marriage. Esther was originally from Brigham and had married Peter Burnyeat of Thurshbank. She had three surviving children and had been widowed for over 30 years - she was now in her mid-seventies. Sarah Pattinson was a little younger, about 65 in 1725, and her husband William had died the year after Esther's Peter. She too had had three young children to bring up. The Pattinsons also lived at Waterend but the family were originally from Clifton. Sarah, however, was definitely a Loweswater woman; she was sister to the younger John Dixon, which made her Ann Dixon's sister-in-law. Both these elderly women probably owed tithes on their widow's third share of their husband's property.

Two of the other women were mother and daughter-in-law, again both widows. Isabell Johnson was probably in her mid-forties; she had been married only four years before her husband, Michael, died leaving her with two children below the age of 3.

Her mother-in-law, Jane (or Jenet) is particularly interesting as her conversion to Quaker beliefs can be dated almost exactly. Jenet's origins are at present unclear but she and Michael Johnson (again of Waterend) married in Loweswater church and baptised their first two children, Janet and Joseph, there. Then in the two years between Joseph's baptism in June 1677 and the birth of their next child, Ruth, in September 1679, Jane and Michael encountered and embraced Quakerism. Ruth's birth and those of her younger brother and sister are noted in Quaker registers.

The only woman whose identity remains uncertain is Mary Wilkinson. The most likely candidate was born Mary Banks in Blindbothel in 1673 and married her first husband, John Wilkinson of, yes, Waterend in 1699 at Pardshaw Meeting House. This marriage was very short-lived - John died seven years after the marriage, aged 45. Mary, 11 years younger than her husband, was left a widow with three young children. Four years later, she married again, to Joseph Bacchus of Broughton Quaker Meeting by whom she had another son, Benjamin, three years later. Of course, this means that in 1725 she would have been known by her second married name, but she was certainly still living at Waterend, the only Mary 'Wilkinson' traceable in the area.

But it was the last and one of the oldest of the women who finally enabled me to date the document to a period of eight weeks. Elizabeth Beeby of Lamplugh in 1676 married Thomas Fletcher of Thrushbank at John Fearon's house at Pardshaw, in the days before the little Meeting House there existed. She bore three children and was widowed sometime before 1710. Records of Friends' House record her burial on 10 January 1726. The list therefore had to be drawn up between 13 November 1725 when the death of Hannah Burnyeat's brother made her an heiress and liable to pay tithes, and early January 1726 when Elizabeth died.

Two interesting conclusions can be drawn from this investigation. One is that, in this admittedly very small sample, it was clearly unusual for widows to remarry even if they were widowed at a very early age. Only one of the eight widows on the list remarried; instead the others coped with managing farms and bringing up young children on their own. This may have been possible because of Quakers' well-developed support system, where Quakers in genuine distress could count of the help of fellow Friends. The unusual independence of Quaker women - they frequently travelled alone and were treated with much more equality than seems the case with non-Quaker women - may also have had some influence. It would be interesting to see if comparable evidence exists for the frequency with which widows did or did not remarry outside the Quaker community and to compare the two.

Secondly, it is clear from identifying these women that the area around and particularly beyond Loweswater lake, from Thrushbank to Iredale Place, including all of the houses in between - the area known collectively as Waterend - was inhabited entirely by Quakers. In many cases the families had been Quaker from the 1670s, only twenty years after Fox's first visit to the county. The Woodvilles held out the longest but the marriage of Ann Dixon's brother, William Woodville in 1705, to another Friend, must have meant that every house in Waterend held a Quaker family. For non-Quakers and the priest at Loweswater, visiting Waterend must have seemed like entering enemy territory. Moreover, in the mid-1720s, almost all the householders were women.

Of the nine women of Waterend who assembled that winter of 1725-6 to speak against tithes, at least five died within the next six years. For the middle-aged and elderly widows, this was hardly surprising but for the young Hannah Burnyeat there was a tragedy in store. In 1729, she married Jacob Fearon and moved to Shatton near Cockermouth to live at Jacob's home. In January 1730, she gave birth to a daughter, who was named after herself and who seems to have thrived. Then disaster, in some unknown shape, struck. Jacob died in January 1731 and two months later, Hannah too was dead. She was 28 years old.

A PLACE OF WOODVILLE'S OWN[1]

The original ownership of such houses as Iredell Place and Jenkinson Place is obvious but 'The Place' is an apparently innocuous name concealing at least two changes of ownership; last century it was Hudson Place and for nearly 200 years before that it was Woodville Place.

The earliest reference (that I can find) to the Woodvilles is the mention of John Wodhall who was on the jury of the Manor Court in 1528. (It was evidently a singularly law-abiding year - the jury had no malefactors to present to the court). The spelling of John's name demonstrates one of the major difficulties in tracing a family whose surname appears in many and varied disguises including: Woodall, Woodell, Wodel, Woadle, Woodvil, Woodle, Woodhall, Woodhalle and even Woodhell.

The first Woodville of whom we know more than his name is another John (most male Woodvilles were John or William). In 1619, this John was amongst 36 tenants of the manor who made an agreement with the Lord, Anthony Patrickson and his son, Henry, in an attempt to settle various disputes that had arisen over the tenants' rights and duties. Amongst other things, the document reveals that the yearly rent for Woodville Place was 9 shillings and 9 pence - the lower side of average for the parish. (Other rents varied from 17s 11d for William Iredell's Fangs to 4s 2d of Peter Burnyeat's home at Pottergill.)

Only one child is definitely recorded as John's - Peter, baptised in 1626 - because the parish registers at this period are incomplete. Fortunately, a will dated 1687 survives in which one William Woodville then resident in the parish of St Cuthbert, Carlisle, obligingly outlines his family.

William, it appears, was also John's son but refers to Peter as his half-brother; it's not clear whether this was by an earlier or later marriage. At the time the will was written, Peter was married and living in Egremont - his inheritance from his brother was £30, by far the most generous single bequest (except for the residue).

Two sisters and another brother are also mentioned in the will. Both sisters were married, and probably living in the Loweswater area. Elizabeth had married a Burnyeat, probably of Mosser, and had four sons (who were left £20 each) and two daughters (left £5 each). Ann had married a Fletcher (possibly of Thrushbank or of Mockerkin) and had two surviving sons and a daughter (left £15 each). William's surviving brother, John, had a daughter who was married to a man in Sunderland and her two sons also were left £15 each.

In addition to these family provisions there were various small bequests: 'to William Graham of Newbiggin forty shillings to buy him a ring

[1] First published April/May 1990.

to wear for my sake'; to an old woman that lives with Thomas Moor, 5d'). William also left a large sum of money - £50 - to the poor of Loweswater parish. The money was to be invested and the interest distributed on St Thomas's Day. Woodville's Charity, as it was known, continued until Victorian days by which time the interest was a very small and useless sum. £30 was similarly left to the poor of Carlisle.

But by far the luckiest beneficiary of William's will was his nephew, son of his brother John. Nephew William, who later inherited the Loweswater house, now inherited the lease of his uncle's house in Carlisle, including all 'bedsteads, cupboards, my silver tankard and my signet, my clock, my napkin, press (cupboard) and all the picters (pictures) and grates and all that is in my closet as it stands and my best horse bridled and sadled and one bedd furnished'. Not a bad inheritance for a boy of eight.

Nephew William was the youngest of five, or possible six, children. (The parish registers are enigmatic.) Only three seem to have survived to adulthood, and by the time William received his inheritance, only he and his elder sister Anne remained at home. In 1630, when William was eleven, Anne - ten years older - created a sensation by running off to Cockermouth to marry John Dixon of Waterend. Not only was John a second-generation Quaker while the Woodvilles were staunchly Anglican, but Anne and John were also too closely related for their marriage to be valid in the eyes of the church - Anne's grandmother was John's aunt. The fact that the Minister at Cockermouth was prepared to marry them suggests that he was probably in ignorance of the facts.

Sixteen years later, William followed his sister's example when he married Sarah Bell, the daughter of another Quaker family. His parents, who continued in the Church of England, were no doubt distressed by the conversion of their only surviving son to Quakerism but, religion aside, Sarah seems to have been all that parents could wish for in a daughter-in-law. Twenty seven years old (the same age as William), she had been orphaned at an early age and was a substantial heiress. Although she had been a little wild in her youth, she grew up to be 'sensitive to the leadings of the Holy Spirit and her conduct became such as to gain her the respect and esteem of Friends'. Later in life she became noted for her quiet encouragement and consolation to those in distress. 'Her few words,' say Quaker records, 'generally had a very tender reach over the meeting'.

After William's father's death in 1714, the couple farmed Woodville Place, played their part in the affairs of the Society of Friends and kept friendly relations with William's sister and her husband at Waterend. Not so friendly, however, were William's relations with a neighbour, John Pattinson, with whom he had a quarrel in 1742, concerning a 'Markstone, formerly set in the waste ground about the tofts'. Other Quakers hastened to mediate.

William and Sarah had five children, four of whom survived to maturity. The oldest, John, married in 1731/2 and, presumably because his father was still farming Woodville Place, moved away. The younger son, William, stayed at home even after he married in 1742 and eventually inherited the property in 1747. Then, for no apparent reason, he bore his wife Jane and their four young children off to Papcastle and leased out Woodville Place. The family never returned to Loweswater.

The family history is too interesting to leave there, however. William died young, at the age of 44, in 1758. His widow sold Woodville Place to the man with whom her husband's father had argued - John Pattinson. The sale price was £708 5s 8d. Jane and her seven children continued to live at Papcastle. One of the sons born in Loweswater, Isaac, married a respectable Quaker girl and settled down to start both a family and a linen drapery business. Another son, William, was particularly intelligent and trained as a doctor in Edinburgh before travelling abroad. All seemed set fair for the family.

Then in January 1778, young William, 26 years old and newly home to set up a doctor's practice in Papcastle, shot dead a man he thought was a burglar. Unfortunately, the burglar turned out to be a respectable young man who was courting Woodville's servant girl. The exact facts are a mystery but it seems likely that William panicked and fired before asking questions. A coroner's jury brought in a verdict of wilful murder but by that time William had fled, via Denbighshire, to London, swearing that he would return to stand his trial. No trial, however, seems ever to have taken place.[1]

Old Jane lived on in Papcastle until her death in 1805. William, in London, obtained an appointment at the St Pancas Smallpox Hospital where he flourished, both in fame and wealth. It was his brother, Isaac, who seems to have suffered most from the affair; only a few months after the shooting, he uprooted his family and took them off to Newcastle upon Tyne. Many Quakers forsook the uncertain country districts of Cumberland for the riches of the thriving town of Newcastle at this period but it is hard to believe that the timing was a coincidence.

In Newcastle, Isaac and his wife Susannah, set up a linen drapery business and enlarged their family to the number of nine. They attended Quaker meetings. Then in 1789, the year his youngest child was born and died, the year of the French Revolution, Isaac went bankrupt. He and his family abruptly disappear from the records. The only later trace I can find of them is a reference to a daughter, Rebecca, inheriting land in Moresby from her mother's brother. What happened to the rest of the family I have

---

[1] William made a great success of his later career as a doctor in London: see *People and Places* for the monument dedicated to him in Boulogne.

yet to discover. There are always more questions to be answered in local history.

Meanwhile, back to the older branch of the family, to the John who went off to farm elsewhere after his marriage in 1731/2. He and his wife, Sarah, seems to have had four children before Sarah died in 1766 'this morning abt 5 a clock', wrote Isaac Fletcher, a diarist and remote relation of the Woodvilles on March 16th. 'Supposed to be mortification of the Bowels occasioned by a fitt of the Cholick to which she is subject'.

Sarah's son, William, had ten children including four sons but only one son, yet another William, survived to old age. He was a tanner by trade, working in Ulverston, and was noted for refusing to travel anywhere - he conducted all his business by post. When he died in the mid-19th century, the male Woodvilles had all died out.

That's presuming, of course, that somewhere in Newcastle or Cumberland, Isaac's sons - William (born 1777 in Cockermouth), John (born 1778 in Cockermouth) and Isaac (born 1786 in Newcastle) had all either died or remained bachelors to the end of their days. Which isn't impossible but - I told you there are always more questions to answer.

Aikbank Mill in Mosser in the 1980s - a corn mill once owned by Quakers and probably serving the Quaker community

Life in old Loweswater

BIBLIOGRAPHY

Besse, Joseph. *A collection of the Sufferings of the people called Quakers for the testimony of a good conscience ...1650 ... to ... 1689.* London, Luke Hinde, 1753
Bolton, John. *Lecture on Lorton and Loweswater 80 years ago.* 1891
Bouch, C M L. *People and Prelates of the Lake Counties.* Kendal, Titus Wilson 1948
Burnyeat, John. *Truth exalted, in the writings of that eminent and faithful servant of Christ, John Burnyeat.* London, Thomas Northcott 1691
Gambles, Robert, *Lake District place-names.* Dalesman, 1980
Housman, John (1764-1802) *A descriptive tour, and guide to the lakes, caves and mountains ...* Carlisle, Jollie 1800
Hutchinson, William (1732-1801) *The history of the county of Cumberland ...* Carlisle, Jollie 1794
Jenkinson, Henry Irwin *Practical guide to the English Lakes. 4th ed.*London, Stanford, 1875
Postlethwaite, John. *Mines and mining in the English Lake District.* Leeds, Samuel Moxon, 1877
Richardson, Sheila & Evans, Pat. *Tales of a Lakeland valley: Loweswater* Workington Mill Field Publications 1996
Southey, Robert *Letters from England: by Don Mauel Alvarez Espriella. Translated from the Spanish* London, Longman 1807
Thompson, Bruce L *The :Lake District and the National Trust* Kendal, Titus Wilson 1946
Whaley, Diana *A dictionary of Lake District place-names.* Nottingham, English place-names society. 2006
Wilson, J (Ed) The *register of the Priory of St Bees.* The Surtees Society cxxvi Durham, Andrews & Co. 1915
Winchester A J L *Landscape and Society in Medieval Cumbria* Edinburgh, John Donald 1987
Winchester, Angus J.L. *Discovering parish boundaries.* Princes Risborough : Shire Publications, 1990
Winchester, Angus J L. Ed. *The diary of Isaac Fletcher of Underwood, Cumberland, 1756-1781* Kendal : Cumberland and Westmorland Antiquarian and Archaeological Society, 1994
Winchester, Angus J L Wordsworth's pure commonwealth, yeoman dynasties in the English Lake District c. 1450-1750 *Armitt Library Journal* 1/1998 pp 86-113

All the items in this bibliography except Wilson, 1915, can be seen by contacting the keeper of the archive of the Lorton & Derwent Fells Local History Society, *www.derwentfells.com* for contact details. The *Newsletter* and *Journal* of the society contain a number of articles covering various other aspects of Loweswater. Wilson, 1915, can be found in the Local Studies Library at Whitehaven Record Office.

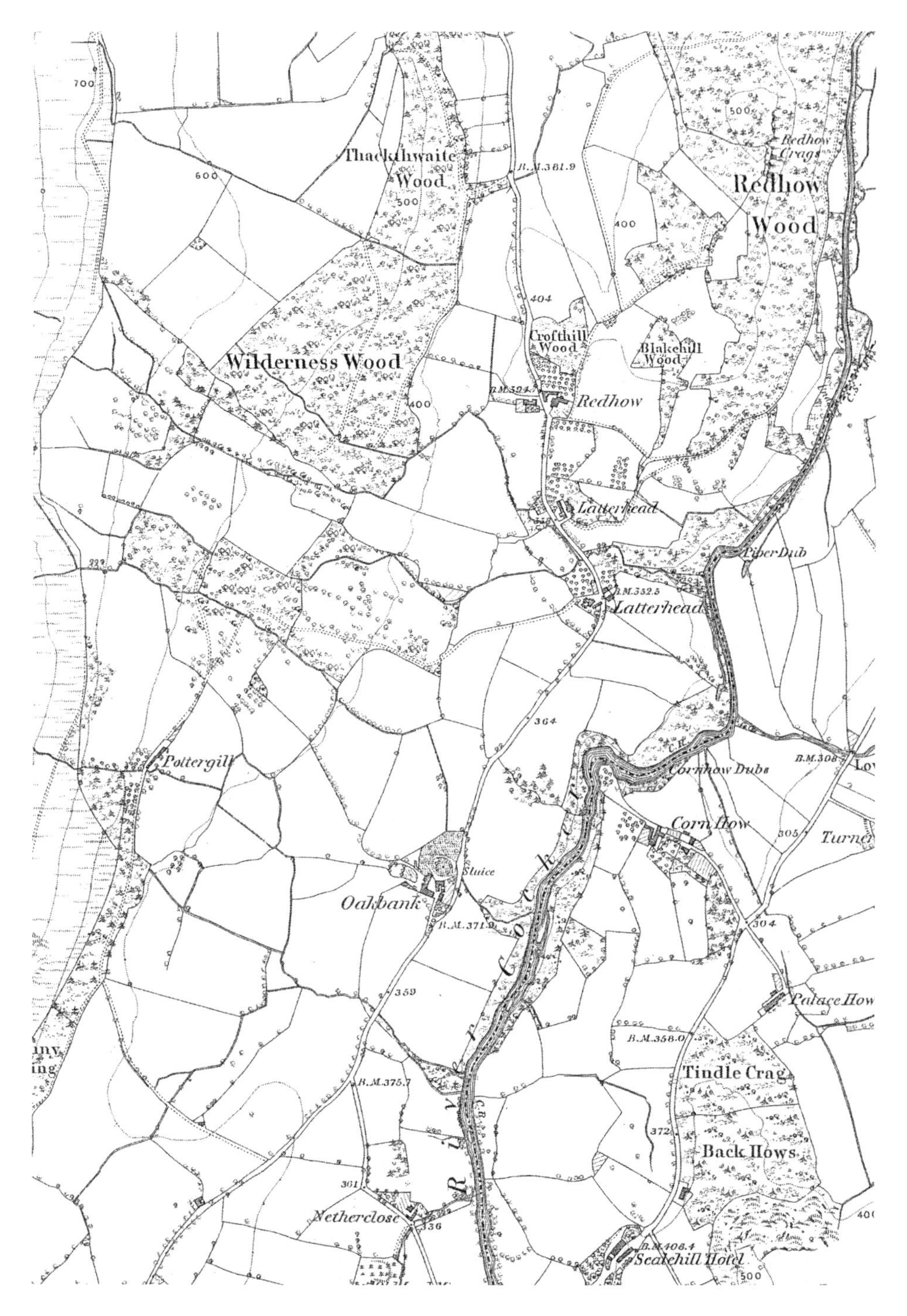

Loweswater, Ordnance Survey 1863 - 6″ to 1 mile: Oakbank/Cold Keld

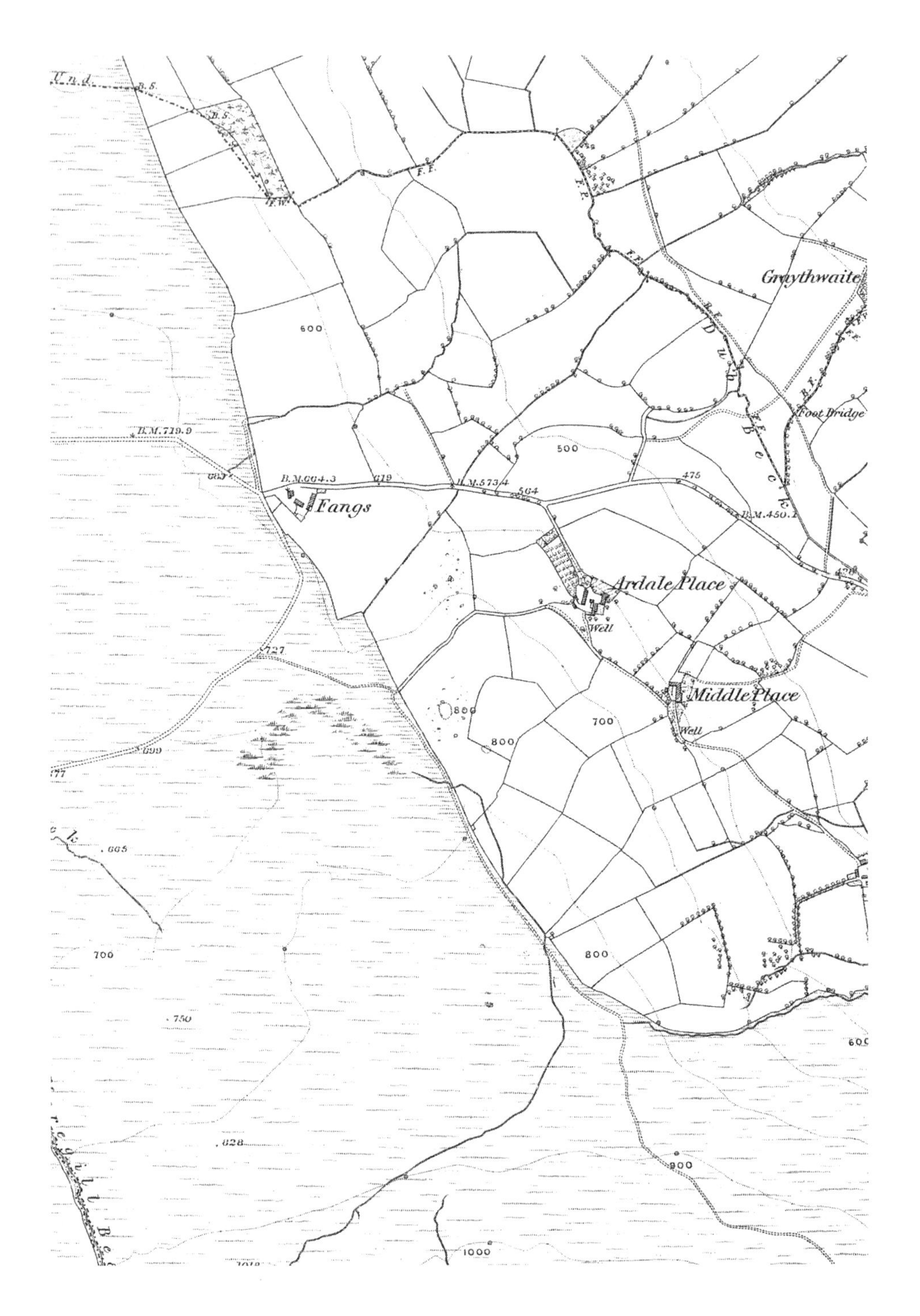

Loweswater, Ordnance Survey 1863 - 6″ to 1 mile: Places west

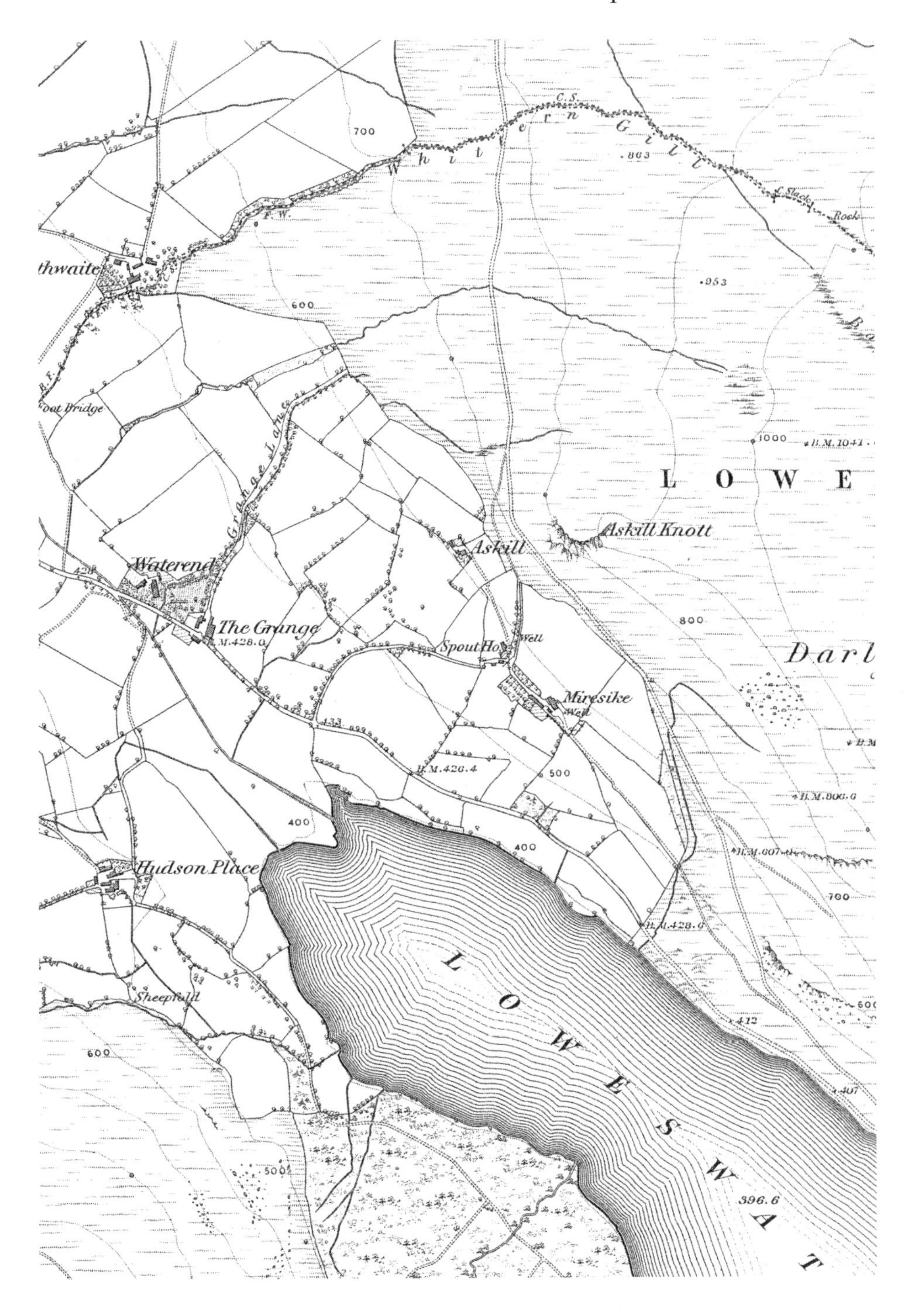

Loweswater, Ordnance Survey 1863 - 6″ to 1 mile: Places east

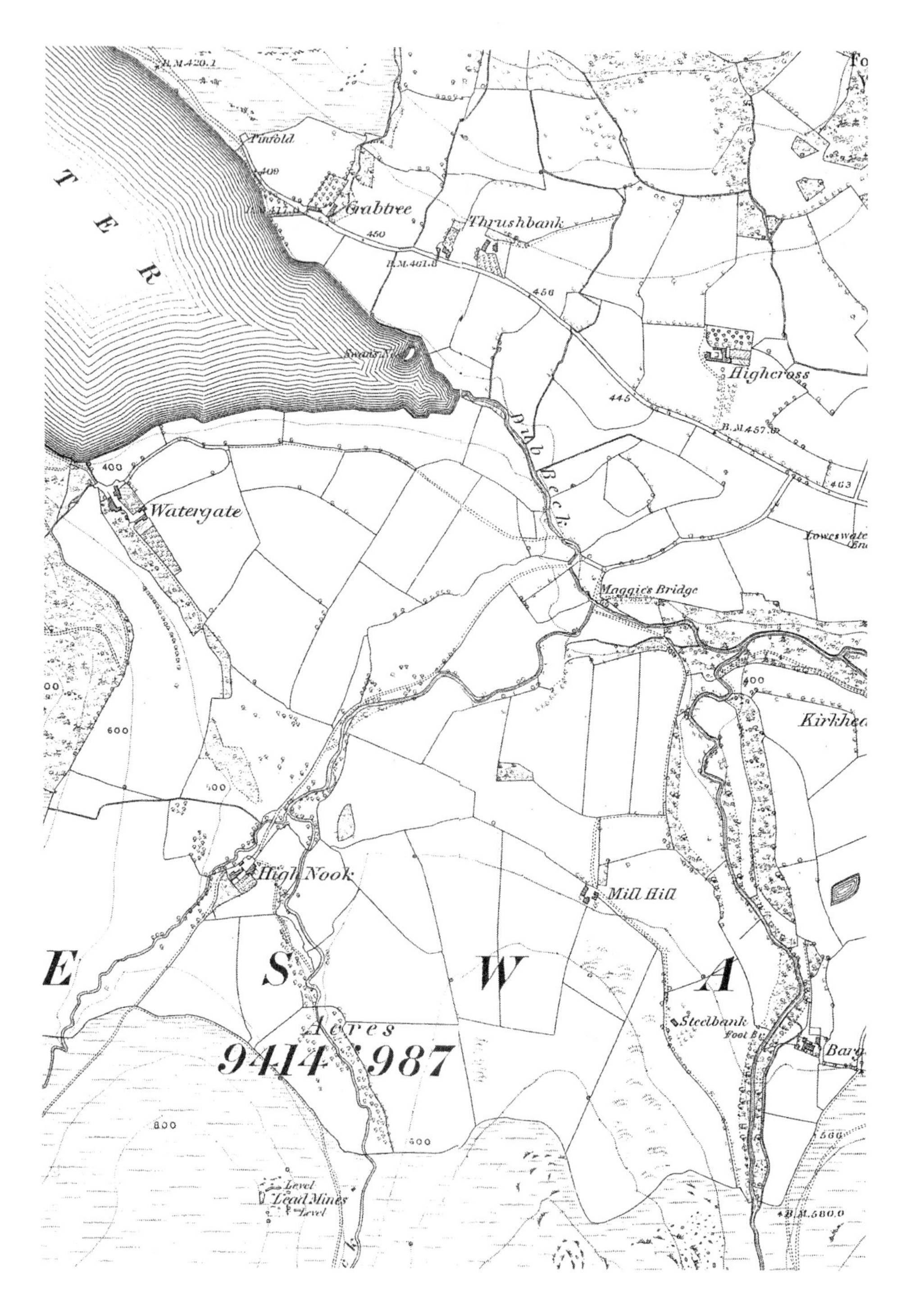

Loweswater, Ordnance Survey 1863 - 6″ to 1 mile: centre west

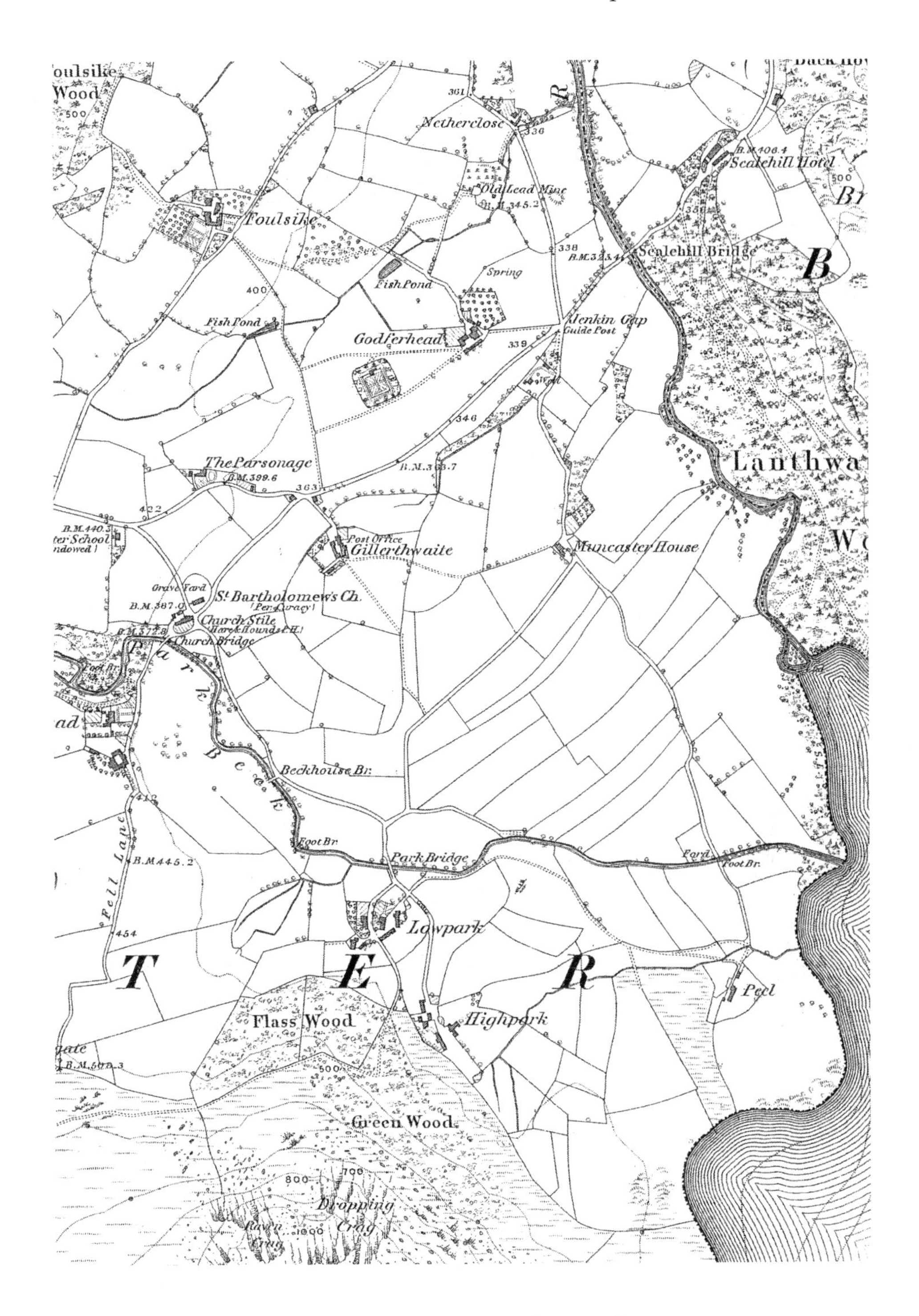

Loweswater, Ordnance Survey 1863 - 6″ to 1 mile: centre west